**32**

# STUDY GUIDE

# The United States, 1919 - 1941

CIE

www.GCSEHistory.com

Published by Clever Lili Limited.

contact@cleverlili.com

First published 2020

ISBN 978-1-913887-31-5

Copyright notice

All rights reserved. No part of this publication may be reproduced in any form or by any means (including photocopying or storing it in any medium by electronic means and whether or not transiently or incidentally to some other use of this publication) with the written permission of the copyright owner. Applications for the copyright owner's written permission should be addressed to the publisher.

Clever Lili has made every effort to contact copyright holders for permission for the use of copyright material. We will be happy, upon notification, to rectify any errors or omissions and include any appropriate rectifications in future editions.

Cover by: Alfred Stieglitz on Wikimedia Commons

Icons by: flaticon and freepik

Contributors: Helen Lamb, Marcus Pailing, Jen Mellors

Edited by Paul Connolly and Rebecca Parsley

Design by Evgeni Veskov and Will Fox

All rights reserved

# DISCOVER MORE OF OUR IGCSE HISTORY STUDY GUIDES
*GCSEHistory.com and Clever Lili*

**STUDY GUIDE 17**
International Relations: Were the Peace Treaties of 1919-23 Fair?

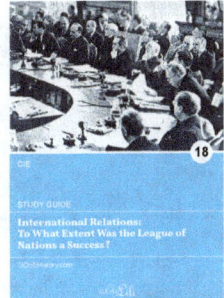
**STUDY GUIDE 18**
International Relations: To What Extent Was the League of Nations a Success?

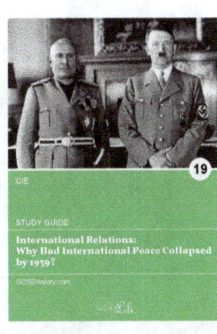
**STUDY GUIDE 19**
International Relations: Why Had International Peace Collapsed by 1939?

**STUDY GUIDE 20**
International Relations: Who Was to Blame for the Cold War?

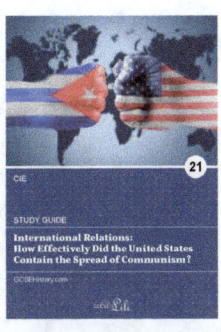
**STUDY GUIDE 21**
International Relations: How Effectively Did the United States Contain the Spread of Communism?

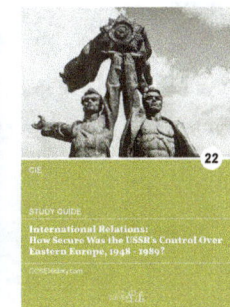
**STUDY GUIDE 22**
International Relations: How Secure Was the USSR's Control Over Eastern Europe, 1948-1989?

**STUDY GUIDE 23**
International Relations: Why Did Events in the Gulf Matter c1970-2000?

**STUDY GUIDE 31**
The First World War, 1914-1918

**STUDY GUIDE 33**
Russia, 1905-1941

**STUDY GUIDE 34**
Germany, 1918-1945

**STUDY GUIDE 46**
China, c1930-1990

## THE GUIDES ARE EVEN BETTER WITH OUR GCSE/IGCSE HISTORY WEBSITE APP AND MOBILE APP

GCSE History is a text and voice web and mobile app that allows you to easily revise for your GCSE/IGCSE exams wherever you are - it's like having your own personal GCSE history tutor. Whether you're at home or on the bus, GCSE History provides you with thousands of convenient bite-sized facts to help you pass your exams with flying colours. We cover all topics - with more than 120,000 questions - across the Edexcel, AQA and CIE exam boards.

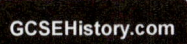

# Contents

How to use this book ................................................................. 5
What is this book about? ........................................................... 6
Revision suggestions ................................................................. 8

## Timelines
The USA, 1919 - 1941 ............................................................... 12

## Background
The USA in 1918 ...................................................................... 14
The US Government ................................................................. 15
The USA in the First World War ............................................... 16
The Cycle of Prosperity ............................................................ 18

## Economic Boom of the Roaring Twenties
The Economic Boom in America .............................................. 18
Advertising ............................................................................... 21
Innovations and Inventions ...................................................... 21
Construction ............................................................................ 22
Mass Production ...................................................................... 22
The Car Industry ...................................................................... 23
Henry Ford ............................................................................... 23
Consumer Goods ..................................................................... 24
The Availability of Credit and Hire Purchase ........................... 24
Consumerism ........................................................................... 25
Electricity and Electrification ................................................... 26
The Stock Market in the 1920s ................................................. 26
The US Government in the 1920s ............................................. 28
Declining Industries ................................................................. 28
Farming in 1920s America ........................................................ 30

## The 'Roaring Twenties'
The Roaring Twenties ............................................................... 31
The Role of Women in 1920s America ..................................... 32
Flappers .................................................................................... 33
Entertainment in 1920s America .............................................. 34
Cinema in 1920s America ......................................................... 35
Sport in 1920s America ............................................................ 35
Jazz in 1920s America .............................................................. 36
Radio in 1920s America ............................................................ 37
Travel in 1920s America ........................................................... 37
Immigration in 1920s America ................................................. 38
The Red Scare of the 1920s ...................................................... 40
The Sacco-Vanzetti Trial .......................................................... 41
The Experience of Black People in 1920s America .................. 43
The Ku Klux Klan in the 1920s ................................................. 44

Religious Divides in 1920s America ......................................... 46
American Fundamentalism ....................................................... 47
American Religious Modernism ............................................... 47
The Scopes Trial, 1925 .............................................................. 48
Prohibition ............................................................................... 49
Al Capone ................................................................................. 51

## Crash and Depression 1929 - 1933
Long-term Weakness in the US Economy During the 1920s .... 52
The Wall Street Crash ............................................................... 53
Effects of the Wall Street Crash ................................................ 54
The Great Depression ............................................................... 54
Farming in 1930s America ........................................................ 55
President Hoover ...................................................................... 56
The Bonus Army Marchers ....................................................... 58

## The New Deal 1933 - 1941
Franklin Delano Roosevelt ....................................................... 59
1932 Election ............................................................................ 59
Fireside Chats ........................................................................... 60
The New Deal and Second New Deal ....................................... 60
The Alphabet Agencies ............................................................. 63
Opposition to the New Deal ..................................................... 65
Huey Long ................................................................................ 67
Father Coughlin ........................................................................ 67
Doctor Townsend ..................................................................... 68
Upton Sinclair .......................................................................... 68
The Success of the New Deal ................................................... 69
Unemployment Figures in Depression America ...................... 71

Glossary .................................................................................... 72
Index ........................................................................................ 75

# HOW TO USE THIS BOOK

In this study guide, you will see a series of icons, highlighted words and page references. The key below will help you quickly establish what these mean and where to go for more information.

## Icons

**WHAT** questions cover the key events and themes.

**WHO** questions cover the key people involved.

**WHEN** questions cover the timings of key events.

**WHERE** questions cover the locations of key moments.

**WHY** questions cover the reasons behind key events.

**HOW** questions take a closer look at the way in which events, situations and trends occur.

**IMPORTANCE** questions take a closer look at the significance of events, situations, and recurrent trends and themes.

**DECISIONS** questions take a closer look at choices made at events and situations during this era.

## Highlighted words

**Abdicate** - occasionally, you will see certain words highlighted within an answer. This means that, if you need it, you'll find an explanation of the word or phrase in the glossary which starts on **page 72**.

## Page references

**Tudor** *(p.7)* - occasionally, a certain subject within an answer is covered in more depth on a different page. If you'd like to learn more about it, you can go directly to the page indicated.

# WHAT IS THIS BOOK ABOUT?

This unit focuses on the USA between the world wars, examining the economic, social and political changes that took place between 1919 and 1941.

## Purpose
The purpose of this course is to investigate the American economy, and the reasons for and consequences of the boom of the 1920s, the Depression of the 1930s, and the significance of the beginning of the Second World War. It also promotes an understanding of social changes across the time period, and the political and economic impact of Roosevelt's New Deal.

## Topics
The course is split into four enquiries:
- The extent to which the US economy boomed in the 1920s, including the reasons for the boom and why some industries benefitted but not others, the lack of prosperity in agriculture and the extent to which all Americans benefitted.
- American social change in the 1920s, including the 'Roaring Twenties', intolerance in society, the introduction and success of Prohibition and the changing role of women.
- The causes and consequences of the Wall Street Crash, including the nature of speculation before the Crash, the impact on the American economy, the social effects and Roosevelt's 1932 election victory.
- The New Deal, including its introduction in 1933, the extent to which it changed during the 1930s, reasons for continuing unemployment, opposition to the New Deal and its overall success.

## Key Individuals
Some of the key individuals studied on this course include:
- Henry Ford.
- Warren Harding.
- Calvin Coolidge.
- Alexander Palmer.
- Johnny Scopes, Clarence Darrow and William J Bryan.
- Nicola Sacco and Bartolomeo Vanzetti.
- Al Capone.
- Herbert Hoover.
- Franklin D Roosevelt.
- Huey Long.
- Father Coughlin.

## Key Events
Some of the key events you will study on this course include:
- The expansion of the US economy in the 1920s.
- Weaknesses in the US economy by the end of the 1920s.
- American society and the 'Roaring Twenties'.
- Intolerance in US society, including the Red Scare, restrictions on immigration, discrimination against black Americans and the rise of the Ku Klux Klan.
- The Wall Street Crash and its financial, social and economic effects.
- The presidential election of 1932.
- Roosevelt's inauguration and the 'Hundred Days'.
- New Deal legislation and the alphabet agencies.
- Opposition to the New Deal, including republican, business radical and Supreme Court opposition.
- Strengths and weaknesses of the New Deal in dealing with unemployment and the Depression.

## WHAT IS THIS BOOK ABOUT?

**Assessment**

The USA 1919 - 1941, is one of the specified depth studies found in Paper 1, where you have a total of 2 hours to complete 3 questions. You must answer 2 questions from the core section of the paper and one question from a choice of two questions on your chosen depth study. Therefore, you will answer one question on The USA 1919 - 1941 if this is your chosen depth study. The question is comprised of 3 sections; a), b), and c).

- Question a is worth 4 marks. This question will require you to describe key features of the time period. You will be asked to recall 2 relevant points and support them with details or provide at least four relevant points without supporting detail.

- Question b is worth 6 marks. This question will require you to explain a key event or development. You will need to identify two reasons, support those reasons with relevant factual detail and then explain how the reasons made the event occur.

- Question c is worth 10 marks. This question will require you to construct an argument to support and challenge an interpretation stated in the question. You will need to have a minimum of three explanations (two on one side and one on the other) in total, fully evaluate the argument and come to a justified conclusion. You will have the opportunity to show your ability to explain and analyse historical events using 2nd order concepts such as causation, consequence, change, continuity, similarity and difference.

- The USA 1919 - 1941 may also appear on Paper 4, a one-hour paper in which you will give an extended answer to one question about this topic. Check with your teacher to find out if you will be taking this option.

# REVISION SUGGESTIONS

Revision! A dreaded word. Everyone knows it's coming, everyone knows how much it helps with your exam performance, and everyone struggles to get started! We know you want to do the best you can in your IGCSEs, but schools aren't always clear on the best way to revise. This can leave students wondering:

- ✓ How should I plan my revision time?
- ✓ How can I beat procrastination?
- ✓ What methods should I use? Flash cards? Re-reading my notes? Highlighting?

Luckily, you no longer need to guess at the answers. Education researchers have looked at all the available revision studies, and the jury is in. They've come up with some key pointers on the best ways to revise, as well as some thoughts on popular revision methods that aren't so helpful. The next few pages will help you understand what we know about the best revision methods.

## How can I beat procrastination?

This is an age-old question, and it applies to adults as well! Have a look at our top three tips below.

### ◎ Reward yourself

When we think a task we have to do is going to be boring, hard or uncomfortable, we often put if off and do something more 'fun' instead. But we often don't really enjoy the 'fun' activity because we feel guilty about avoiding what we should be doing. Instead, get your work done and promise yourself a reward after you complete it. Whatever treat you choose will seem all the sweeter, and you'll feel proud for doing something you found difficult. Just do it!

### ◎ Just do it!

We tend to procrastinate when we think the task we have to do is going to be difficult or dull. The funny thing is, the most uncomfortable part is usually making ourselves sit down and start it in the first place. Once you begin, it's usually not nearly as bad as you anticipated.

### ◎ Pomodoro technique

The pomodoro technique helps you trick your brain by telling it you only have to focus for a short time. Set a timer for 20 minutes and focus that whole period on your revision. Turn off your phone, clear your desk, and work. At the end of the 20 minutes, you get to take a break for five. Then, do another 20 minutes. You'll usually find your rhythm and it becomes easier to carry on because it's only for a short, defined chunk of time.

## Spaced practice

We tend to arrange our revision into big blocks. For example, you might tell yourself: "This week I'll do all my revision for the Cold War, then next week I'll do the Medicine Through Time unit."

# REVISION SUGGESTIONS

This is called **massed practice**, because all revision for a single topic is done as one big mass.

But there's a better way! Try **spaced practice** instead. Instead of putting all revision sessions for one topic into a single block, space them out. See the example below for how it works.

This means planning ahead, rather than leaving revision to the last minute - but the evidence strongly suggests it's worth it. You'll remember much more from your revision if you use **spaced practice** rather than organising it into big blocks. Whichever method you choose, though, remember to reward yourself with breaks.

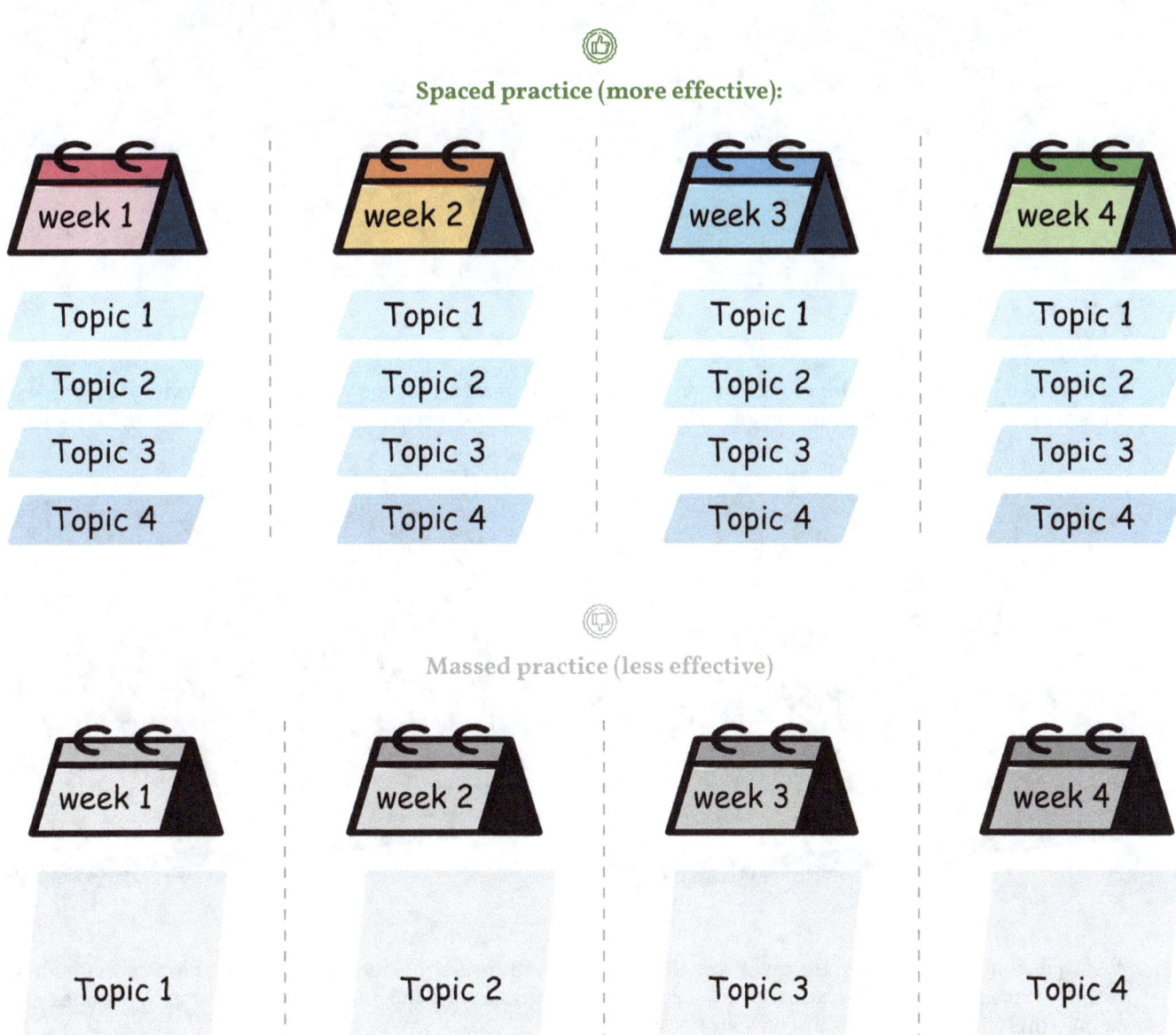

# REVISION SUGGESTIONS

 **What methods should I use to revise?**

Self-testing/flash cards

Self explanation/mind-mapping

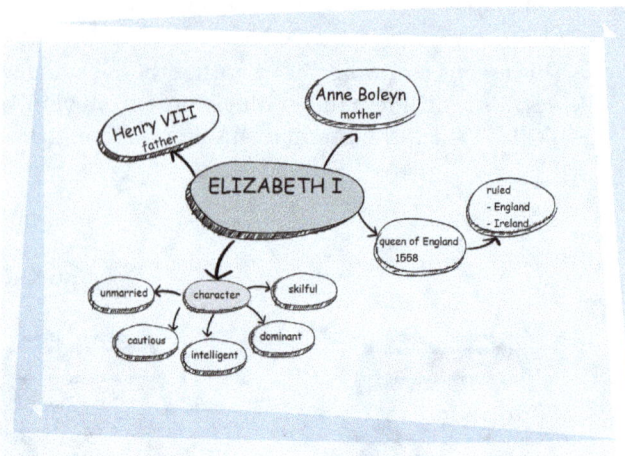

The research shows a clear winner for revision methods - **self-testing**. A good way to do this is with **flash cards**. Flash cards are really useful for helping you recall short – but important – pieces of information, like names and dates.

Side A - question

Side B - answer

Write questions on one side of the cards, and the answers on the back. This makes answering the questions and then testing yourself easy. Put all the cards you get right in a pile to one side, and only repeat the test with the ones you got wrong - this will force you to work on your weaker areas.

pile with right answers

pile with wrong answers

As this book has a quiz question structure itself, you can use it for this technique.

Another good revision method is **self-explanation**. This is where you explain how and why one piece of information from your course linked with another piece.

This can be done with **mind-maps**, where you draw the links and then write explanations for how they connect. For example, President Truman is connected with anti-communism because of the Truman Doctrine.

## REVISION SUGGESTIONS

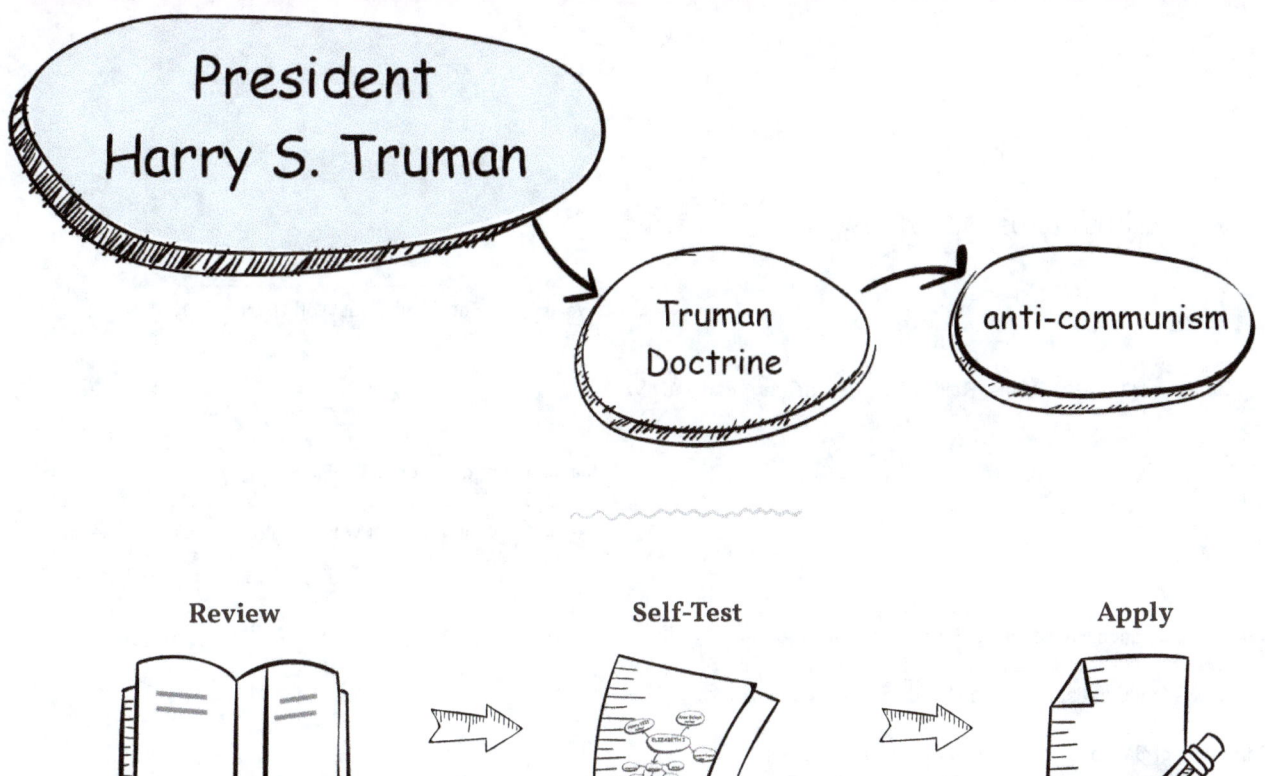

Start by highlighting or re-reading to create your flashcards for self-testing.

Test yourself with flash cards. Make mind maps to explain the concepts.

Apply your knowledge on practice exam questions.

 **Which revision techniques should I be cautious about?**

**Highlighting** and **re-reading** are not necessarily bad strategies - but the research does say they're less effective than flash cards and mind-maps.

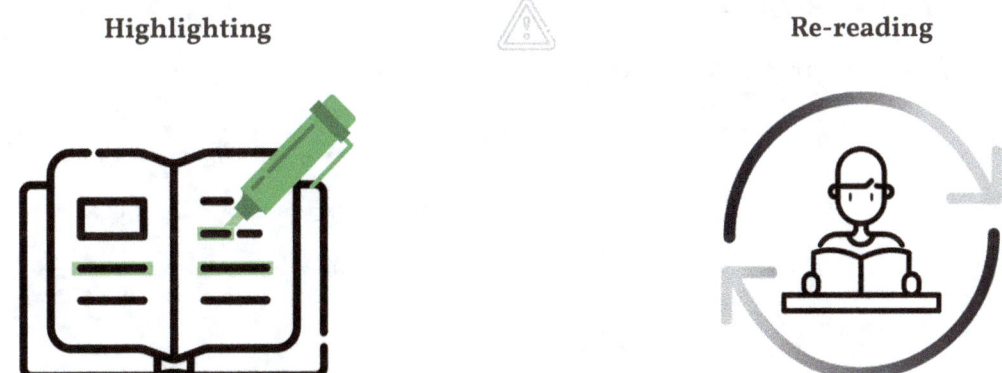

If you do use these methods, make sure they are **the first step to creating flash cards**. Really engage with the material as you go, rather than switching to autopilot.

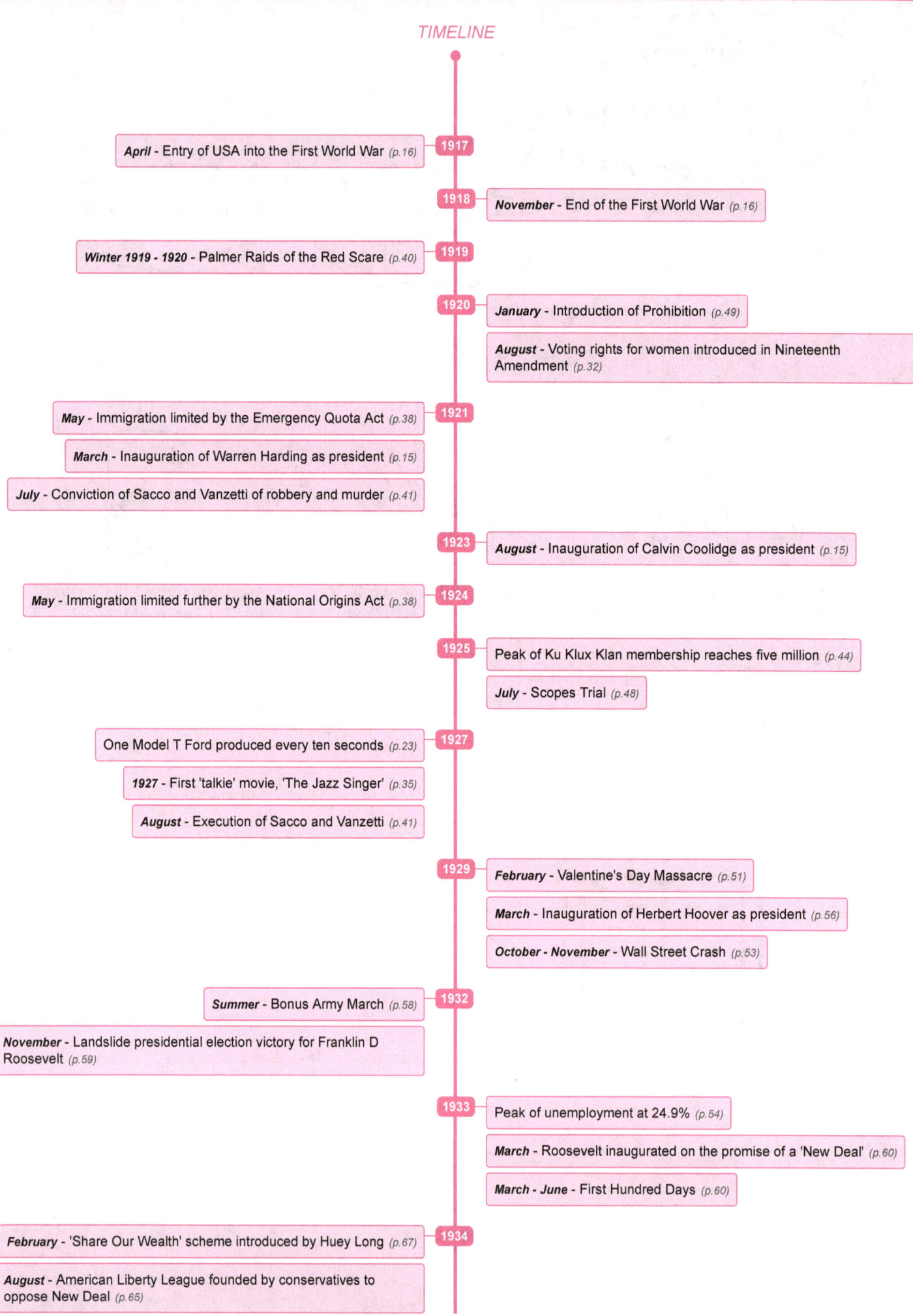

# THE USA, 1919 - 1941

*November* - National Union for Social Justice introduced by Father Coughlin *(p.67)*

**1935**

*May* - NRA declared unconstitutional by Supreme Court *(p.65)*

*May* - Roosevelt presents his Second New Deal *(p.60)*

*September* - Assassination of Huey Long *(p.67)*

**1936**

*January* - AAA declared unconstitutional by Supreme Court *(p.65)*

*November* - Second landslide election victory for Roosevelt *(p.59)*

*November* - Threat by Roosevelt to 'pack' the Supreme Court *(p.65)*

**1939**

*September* - Start of Second World War *(p.69)*

**1941**

*December* - USA enters the war following the Pearl Harbor bombing *(p.71)*

# THE USA IN 1918

*'I believe in America... because we have great dreams and because we have the opportunity to make those dreams come true.'*
Wendell Willkie

### What was America like in 1918?
At the end of the First World War, America was a large country made up of 48 states. It was rich in natural resources, experiencing rapid industrialisation, and had a young and diverse population.

### How big was the USA in 1918?
In 1918, America spread across 9 million square miles. It stretched from Canada to Mexico, and from the Atlantic to the Pacific Ocean.

### What was the size of the US population in 1918?
About 109 million people lived in America in 1918.

### Who lived in America in 1918?
In 1918, people living in the USA came from a variety of backgrounds:
- Europeans, Latin Americans and Asians continued to emigrate to the country throughout the 19th and early 20th centuries.
- Many African-Americans lived there because their ancestors had been brought there as slaves.
- Many of the longer-standing immigrants, whose families had lived in America for generations, were known as White Anglo-Saxon Protestants, or WASPs.
- Native Americans, whose ancestors had lived in America before the settlers, also lived there.

### Who experienced racism in America in 1918?
In the mixed cultural heritage of the USA in 1918, some groups experienced prejudice, racism and disadvantages.
- Slavery didn't end until after the end of the American Civil War, in 1865, and African-Americans continued to experience racism and inequality.
- Immigration laws were passed to reduce the number of immigrants in the late 19th and early 20th centuries, particularly from certain countries.
- Native Americans were forced to live on reservations as their lands had been taken over by settlers.

### What natural resources did America have in 1918?
In 1918 the USA was rich in a number of natural resources:
- Timber.
- Coal.
- Iron.
- Gold and silver.
- Oil reserves.
- Farmland, which was used to grow crops such as wheat, corn, tobacco and cotton.
- Workers - America had a young and growing population to work in its industries.

> **DID YOU KNOW?**
>
> **The United States became an independent country on 4th July, 1776, with the Declaration of Independence.**
>
> This is why Americans celebrate 4th July as Independence Day.

# THE US GOVERNMENT

*'To live under the American Constitution is the greatest political privilege that was ever accorded the human race.'*
*President Calvin Coolidge*

### How does the American government work?

The USA is a democracy and a republic. Its government is defined by the constitution, which sets out how it should be run.

### What role does the constitution play in the American government?

The constitution is a set of laws that define how America is run. It is seen as having the highest authority in any government.

### How is the constitution amended in the American government?

The American constitution is designed to be difficult to amend. There are 2 main ways it can be done.

- Congress has to pass the amendment with a two-thirds majority in both houses. It then has to be approved by three quarters of all state legislatures.
- A constitutional convention can be called to draft an amendment if desired by two thirds of all states. This method has never been used.

### What does unconstitutional mean in the American government?

Anything that breaks the laws of the constitution is said to be unconstitutional and can not legally exist.

### What were the powers of the American government in 1918?

Law-making powers were shared between the federal (central) and state governments in 3 main ways:

- The federal government in Washington DC was responsible for foreign policy, war, trade between states and the currency.
- The state governments were responsible for education, marriage laws, trade within the state and local government.
- The federal and state governments shared control of law and order, the courts, taxes, banks, and public welfare.

### How was the American government structured?

Power in the federal government was divided between 3 branches - the executive (president), legislature (Congress) and judiciary (courts).

- The president (executive) suggested laws, ran foreign policy and the army, and appointed government ministers.
- Congress (legislature) was split into two houses: the Senate and the House of Representatives. They passed laws, agreed taxes and endorsed the president's appointments of judges and ministers.

- The Supreme Court (the judiciary) interpreted laws and the constitution and was the highest court of appeal for people to question decisions by the government and courts.

### What checks and balances are there in the American government?

The US government was arranged to make sure no single group could take over or have too much power over the others in 4 main ways:
- The president could veto laws by Congress, but Congress could override the veto with a two-thirds majority. Congress could also withhold taxes or stop the president from appointing judges or ministers.
- The president could appoint judges for the Supreme Court, but the Supreme Court could stop the president's actions if it decided they were unconstitutional.
- Congress could override Supreme Court judgements by passing amendments to change the constitution, but the Supreme Court could say Congress's other laws were unconstitutional.
- Congress could remove a president from office due to acts of treason, bribery or another high crime; this is known as impeachment.

### Which political parties were there in the American government in 1918?

By 1918, there were 2 main political parties in America:
- The Republicans, who wanted businesses to succeed.
- The Democrats, who wanted a solution to America's social problems.

### How do state governments work within the American government?

Like the federal government, state governments were divided into executive, legislature and judicial branches.
- The executive branch was headed by a governor, elected by the people.
- The legislature usually had two houses, a Senate and a House of Representatives, to vote on laws and the state budget.
- The state judicial branch was led by the state Supreme Court.

**DID YOU KNOW?**

The American Constitution contains 4534 words.

# THE USA IN THE FIRST WORLD WAR

*'Standing on the brink of this terrible vortex...'*
George Norris, 1917

### How did the First World War affect the USA?

America didn't join the First World War until 1917, but the war was to have a massive social and economic impact. America experienced benefits as well as problems as a result of the war.

### What was the American economy like before the USA joined the First World War?

Before the First World War, American industry was thriving. By 1900 it was competing with other industrialised countries to produce and sell the most lucrative goods, such as oil, coal and textiles.

### When did the USA join the First World War?
America joined the First World War on 6th April, 1917.

### Why did America join the Allies in the First World War in 1917?
The USA avoided taking sides when the First World War broke out in 1914. However, it was pushed to ally with Britain and France in 1917 following 4 key events:
- After war broke out, America began lending money to Britain and France, and selling them more goods than it sold to Germany.
- Public opinion in the USA was strong against reported German atrocities in Belgium.
- German U-boats began to attack and sink American ships, including the passenger ship Lusitania in 1915.
- In 1917, a secret telegram revealed a German plot to use Mexico against the USA, which lead to the outbreak of war.

### Why did the First World War benefit America?
European countries in the war couldn't produce as many goods, so they sold less and bought more. Because it was a long way from the fighting, America made money from providing the goods that were needed.

### What economic benefits did America see from the First World War?
America benefitted economically from the First World War in 9 key ways:
- American banks had loaned nearly $10 billion to European countries for war costs and rebuilding by 1919.
- War economies in European countries meant that they relied more on buying American goods.
- Countries around the world were also more likely to buy American goods as European industrial production slowed down.
- Factory production grew by 35%.
- There was more demand for steel.
- Coal, petrol and gas production grew.
- Shipbuilders had to replace ships that were sunk by submarines.
- The American railway network was modernised to transport troops and goods around the country.
- American consumer goods became popular in Europe.

### How did American agriculture benefit from the First World War?
Farmers benefitted from the First World War because European countries couldn't grow or sell food while there was fighting, so there was greater demand for American crops.
- Food prices rose by 25%.
- Farmers could afford to buy machinery such as tractors.
- Many farmers borrowed money and bought more land to grow the food that was needed.

### What problems did the First World War cause for America?
The war caused some problems in America, particularly in the months after it ended.
- 100,000 American soldiers had died fighting.
- Returning soldiers went back into the workplace. Some couldn't find jobs and others took those that had been done by women, throwing them out of work in turn.
- The increased use of black workers during the war caused race riots at the end of it.
- Demand for goods dropped as Europe began to produce its own goods again.
- The demand for food dropped as Europe began to grow more food again. Food prices dropped and farmers struggled to pay off the money they had borrowed.

### DID YOU KNOW?

America loaned nearly $10 billion to other countries during and immediately after the First World War.

# THE CYCLE OF PROSPERITY

*'After all, the chief business of the American people is business.'*
Calvin Coolidge, 1925

### What is a cycle of prosperity?
During the 1920s the USA entered the cycle of prosperity. This happens when different parts of the economy boost each other and help each other to grow.

### How does more money lead to the cycle of prosperity?
When they have more money, people want to buy more. Demand for goods rises.

### How does more demand lead to the cycle of prosperity?
In order to meet increased demand, factories make more goods and production rises.

### How does more production lead to the cycle of prosperity?
To produce more goods, factories need to employ more people and pay them.

### How does more work lead to the cycle of prosperity?
When more people are being paid for working more hours, they have more money, and the cycle continues.

### DID YOU KNOW?

**Rising wages fuelled the economic boom.**
In 1919, the average industrial worker would earn $1,158 in a year. By 1929, the average annual wage was $1,304.

# THE ECONOMIC BOOM IN AMERICA

*'We in America are nearer to the financial triumph over poverty than ever before.'*
Herbert Hoover, 1928

### What was the economic boom in 1920s America?
During the 1920s the American economy grew so rapidly that it became known as the 'boom'. Wealth increased and businesses became much bigger.

### What is an economic boom?
An economic boom is when the wealth and prosperity of a country grows very quickly. Businesses make more profit and expand, and the standard of living rises. The cycle of prosperity *(p.18)* begins.

### Why was there more money during the economic boom of the 1920s?
A number of circumstances meant that more Americans had more money to spend.
- The GDP of the USA increased by 40% between 1922 and 1929.
- The average wage had increased by 8% between 1920 and 1929.
- Ordinary people made money buying stocks and shares.
- More credit *(p.24)* meant that there was more money available to borrow.

### Why was there more demand for goods during the economic boom of the 1920s?
Demand increased, which meant that people wanted to buy more. This was caused by various changes in 1920s America.
- Advertising encouraged Americans to 'keep up with the Joneses', and to buy the latest goods to improve their social standing.
- Companies provided for a consumer society, producing more varieties and newer versions of goods to stimulate demand and encourage people to buy.
- Consumer goods such as vacuum cleaners, radios and gramophones, were invented and mass produced. With electricity *(p.26)* in their homes, more Americans could use these.
- Mass production *(p.22)* meant that goods were cheaper, so more people could afford to buy them, and wanted to do so.
- Hire purchase (paying in instalments) made goods more affordable, and increased the number of people who wanted to buy them.

### Why was there more production during the economic boom of the 1920s?
During the 1920s, production in America increased dramatically. This was the result of a variety of changes.
- Mass production *(p.22)* techniques such as standardisation, division of labour and moving assembly lines meant that more goods could be made.
- The use of electricity *(p.26)* in factories helped to increase production.
- The money given to companies through the sales of stocks and shares allowed them to increase their capacity for production.

### Why did employment increase during the economic boom of the 1920s?
In 1920s America there were more jobs available, and more people were able to find work. This was the result of several factors:
- Workers were employed so that factories could meet the demand for the new consumer goods.
- The car industry *(p.23)* became enormous, with four million workers employed in it by 1929.
- The mass production *(p.22)* of consumer goods had a knock-on effect on other industries that produced the materials needed. For example, more cars led to more jobs in the steel, glass and rubber industries.
- New industries provided many jobs. One example is the advertising industry, which employed 600,000 people by the end of the 1920s.
- People had more leisure time. This led to more jobs being created within the service and entertainment industries.
- Workers were employed to build 400,000 km of roads across America.

### Who didn't benefit from the economic boom of the 1920s?
An estimated 60% of Americans lived below the poverty line during the 1920s, and didn't benefit from the economic boom. Some groups in particular were economically vulnerable:

- Many African Americans worked in agriculture in the southern states, with unstable employment and extreme poverty. Those who moved north found that there were few employment opportunities for them in the cities, and they had to work in low-paid jobs such as domestic service and casual labouring.
- Native Americans lived on reservations with poor soil, poor education and few opportunities. Those who left found that employment opportunities were limited to low-paid and casual work.
- New immigrants suffered from discrimination, especially if they were Jewish or Catholic. Often, only the lowest-paid jobs were available to them.
- Workers in declining industries, such as coal and textiles, saw their wages fall and did not benefit from the boom.
- Casual and unskilled workers were less likely to benefit from the boom.
- Farmers and other agricultural workers didn't benefit.

### How was wealth distributed during the economic boom of the 1920s?

The wealth became even more unevenly distributed in the USA, and many Americans didn't benefit from it.

### How many people benefitted from the economic boom of the 1920s?

78% of the profits made in the 1920s belonged to just 0.3% of the population.

### How many lived in poverty during the economic boom of the 1920s?

An estimated 18 million Americans lived in poverty in in the 1920s.

### How many were unemployed during the economic boom of the 1920s?

Approximately two million people were unemployed at the end of the 1920s.

### Which industries didn't benefit from the economic boom of the 1920s?

Although many industries thrived in America in the 1920s, others went into decline, and their workers suffered lower wages and higher unemployment. These included:

- Agriculture.
- The textiles industry.
- Coal mining.
- Shipbuilding.
- Railways.

**DID YOU KNOW?**

**The 1920s offered some Americans the opportunity to prosper.**

In 1914 there were about 7,000 millionaires in America. By 1929, there were 35,000.

# ADVERTISING

*'Remember, your teeth get no vacation.'*
*Colgate advert, 1924*

### What was the effect of mass marketing in America in the 1920s?
The growth of advertising (sometimes known as mass marketing) in the 1920s boosted the US economy.

### How did advertising improve the economy in 1920s America?
Advertisements encouraged people to buy more goods and boosted sales.

### How did radio affect advertising in 1920s America?
Radio advertising became popular, and advertisers used entertainment to sell their goods. This meant that people spent more leisure time listening to adverts.

### How did advertising affect employment in 1920s America?
The advertising industry employed more workers. 600,000 Americans worked in advertising by 1929.

### How did advertising affect society in 1920s America?
Advertising helped to create a consumer society, in which people were encouraged to buy even more goods and to prioritise possessions and shopping more.

> **DID YOU KNOW?**
>
> The first radios to be sold as household appliances were known as 'radiolas'.
> They cost $75 in 1922.

# INNOVATIONS AND INVENTIONS

*'I was trying to make something really hard, but then I thought I should make something really soft instead, that could be molded into different shapes. That was how I came up with the first plastic. I called it Bakelite.'*
*Leo Baekeland*

### What was the effect of inventions in 1920s America?
At the end of the war various products and methods of production were developed.

### Which inventions improved communications in 1920s America?
Dial phones, coin phones, teletype machines and the automatic switchboard all improved communications.

### What new materials were invented in 1920s America?
New synthetic materials were developed by the chemical industry, such as cellophane, rayon, nylon and bakelite.

**Which inventions improved the building industry in 1920s America?**
Pneumatic drills and concrete mixers sped up the building industry and made it more efficient.

> **DID YOU KNOW?**
> Nylon is named for the cities of New York (ny) and London (lon).

# CONSTRUCTION

*'The Empire State Building is the closest thing to heaven in this city'.*
*Terry McKay in An Affair to Remember, played by Deborah Kerr*

**What was the effect of construction on the economic boom of 1920s America?**
During the 1920s, the construction industry thrived as it built new shops, factories and offices for new businesses, as well as roads, homes, hospitals and schools. Skyscrapers, such as the Empire State Building, became a familiar sight in cities.

# MASS PRODUCTION

*'You can have any colour as long as it's black.' Henry Ford, 1908*

**What was mass production in America?**
Mass production involved innovations and techniques that made it quicker, easier and cheaper to make goods in factories.

**What was mass production in 1920s America?**
Mass production meant that goods cost less to make. This meant that they could be sold more cheaply, which increased demand.

**How did mass production work?**
Mass production involved several stages.

- ✅ Standardisation meant that all the parts used to make goods were the same size and shape.
- ✅ Division of labour meant that each worker performed the same task over and over again.
- ✅ A moving assembly line meant that the workers stayed still while the goods were brought to them to work on.

> **DID YOU KNOW?**
> **Mass production techniques meant goods could be produced faster.**
> In 1927, one Model T Ford was produced every 10 seconds.

22 — Quizzes, amazing exam preparation tools and more at GCSEHistory.com

# THE CAR INDUSTRY

*'We'd rather do without clothes than the car.'*
*A mother of nine, speaking in 1924*

### What was the car industry in 1920s America?
The growth of the car industry in 1920s America offered the country more opportunities for economic growth, as well as accelerating great social change.

### How many cars were produced in 1920s America?
By 1929 there were 26 million cars on the road in America, which had a massive impact on society at the time.

### Why was Henry Ford important to mass production in the car industry?
Henry Ford *(p.23)* was an American industrialist and owner of Ford Motor Company. He developed effective mass production *(p.22)* techniques that made it quicker and cheaper to make cars.

### What was the effect of the car industry on the 1920s economy in America?
Cheaper, mass-produced cars had a knock-on effect on other parts of the American economy.
- Sales of steel, rubber, glass and textiles increased, because they were needed to make the cars. 20% of US steel and 75% of US glass were used to make cars.
- More cars meant that more roads were built.
- More cars meant that oil sales increased, and there were more jobs for mechanics.
- Because people could travel, there were more hotels, roadside diners and petrol stations, all of which needed workers.
- People were able to drive to work, and so lived further away in the suburbs. This led to more demand for house-building.
- It became easier to travel to isolated rural areas, and they became better connected.

> **DID YOU KNOW?**
>
> **Mass production meant goods were more widely available and cheaper than previously.**
>
> In 1929 there was one car for every five Americans, compared to one car for every 43 British people.

# HENRY FORD

*'If you think you can do a thing, or think you can't do a thing, you're right.'*
*Henry Ford*

### Who was Henry Ford?
Henry Ford owned Ford Motor Company. His factory in Detroit became the largest in the world.

### How did Henry Ford treat his workers?
Workers at Ford were comparatively well-paid. However, many of them had to promise not to join a trade union.

### What was Ford's assembly line?
Ford developed the assembly line and conveyor belt to speed up motor production. As production got faster, the price of the car fell. As a result, 15 million people bought Model T Fords between 1911 and 1929.

> **DID YOU KNOW?**
>
> Henry Ford was America's second billionaire.

# CONSUMER GOODS

*'What is the first condition of our civilization? ...is it not concerned with the production of things?'*
Samuel Strauss, 1923

### What were consumer goods in 1920s America?
Consumer goods were items that customers wanted, rather than needed. New technology and mass production *(p.22)* techniques meant that these became more available in 1920s America.

### What were consumer goods in 1920s America?
There were many different examples of new consumer goods in 1920s America.
- Vacuum cleaners.
- Radios.
- Hair dryers.
- Refrigerators.
- Gramophones.

> **DID YOU KNOW?**
>
> **Consumerism was fuelled by the rise of the leisure industry.**
> It cost between 10 and 20 cents to visit the cinema. Films showcased fabulous lifestyles and the latest consumer goods.

# THE AVAILABILITY OF CREDIT AND HIRE PURCHASE
*Why pay cash?*

### What was the role of credit in America in the 1920s?
Credit became more available in the 1920s. This meant that banks and businesses were more prepared to lend people money to buy the goods that they wanted.

### What was hire purchase as a form of credit?
Hire purchase meant that people could buy goods without paying in full straight away. Instead, they could take the item home after paying a deposit, and pay the rest of the cost in instalments.

### How was credit used for 'buying on the margin'?
'Buying on the margin' was when the banks gave people credit to use to buy shares with just a 10% deposit, known as 'the margin'. They were expected to pay this back when they had sold their shares at a profit.

### What was the effect of hire purchase and credit in 1920s America?
Hire purchase and credit increased demand and the sale of goods, as it made them more affordable and available to ordinary people.

> **DID YOU KNOW?**
> Consumer debt more than doubled between the 1920s and 1930s.

## CONSUMERISM
*'We are urged on the highest authority to spend rather than to save.'*
*Stuart Chase, 1929*

### What was consumerism?
Consumerism is the idea that people should buy more. America became a consumer society where people were encouraged to shop. Companies came up with wider varieties of goods and new ideas to persuade people to buy them.

### Why did America become a consumer society in the 1920s?
By the 1920s, America had become a 'consumer society'. There were a number of reasons for this.
- ✓ Consumer goods were invented and mass produced. These were goods that people wanted rather than needed.
- ✓ The growth in advertising encouraged people to buy more. They told people to 'keep up with the Joneses', and shop in order to increase their social standing.
- ✓ Businesses encouraged consumerism by producing more varieties, more disposable items and newer, better consumer goods.
- ✓ New sales methods and businesses were developed.

### How did consumerism change the sales industry?
The new consumerist society both caused and was impacted by the development of new sales methods and businesses.
- ✓ The number of mail-order companies, such as Sears, Roebuck and Company, grew. This meant even those living in remote areas could buy goods from catalogues.
- ✓ Travelling salesmen could use roads to cover a wider area and increase their sales.
- ✓ Chain stores, which belonged to the same company and sold the same goods, began to spread across America.
- ✓ Hire purchase and credit *(p.24)* made goods more affordable.
- ✓ The growth in advertising led to an increase in demand.

### How did consumerism boost the economy?

Consumerism contributed to the economic boom.

- ✓ The culture of consumerism meant that people wanted to buy more and better goods, so it increased demand and sales.
- ✓ There was more confidence in the economy. People were more likely to spend money, rather than saving it.

**DID YOU KNOW?**

**Advertising was used to boost demand.**
In 1929, American industry spent $3 billion on advertising.

# ELECTRICITY AND ELECTRIFICATION

*'Miss Electricity' is queen of all she surveys*

### How did electricity boost the economy?

During the 1920s, the US electricity grid was widened to include many homes and businesses. This made factories more efficient and allowed people to buy and use more consumer goods, which ran on electricity.

### What was the impact of electricity?

Electricity benefitted the economy in a number of ways.

- ✓ With their homes on the grid, people were able to use consumer goods that ran on electricity. This increased demand for them.
- ✓ Factories could use electricity to run more efficiently. This increased production.
- ✓ Electricity powered the radios that advertised products, leading to increased demand for goods.

**DID YOU KNOW?**

**Electricity was used to power consumer goods in people's homes**
By 1929, nearly 68% of American homes were electrified.

# THE STOCK MARKET IN THE 1920S

*'I am firm in my belief that anyone not only can be rich, but ought to be rich.'*
John J Raskob, 1929

### What are shares?

A share is part-ownership in a company. Buying shares is a way in which people can invest in businesses.

### What is a shareholder?
Businesses sell shares, which are bought by shareholders. The money is used by the business to expand and increase production.

### What are the dividends of shares?
When the business has made a profit, it gives some of it to shareholders. This is known as a dividend.

### How does the stock market relate to shares?
The stock market is a place to buy and sell shares, and it decides how much each share is worth.

### What affected share value in 1920s America?
In 1920s America, 2 main factors affected the value of shares:
- ✓ The performance of the company, how well it was doing, and how much profit it was expected to make.
- ✓ The demand for shares. The more people who wanted to buy shares in a particular company, the higher the price of the shares.

### How did the buying of shares change in the 1920s?
During the 1920s, there were a number of changes to the way that shares were bought and sold.
- ✓ Before the 1920s, people usually bought shares to keep, making their money from dividends. However, share prices rose so much in the 1920s that people starting speculating - buying shares to sell at a profit.
- ✓ More people bought shares, hoping to 'get rich quick' through speculation. In 1920, one in twenty Americans was a shareholder, but by 1929 it was one in six.
- ✓ Before the 1920s, shares tended to be bought and sold by rich people and banks. However, during the decade it became more common for ordinary people to speculate as well.
- ✓ During the 1920s, banks began to lend people money to speculate with. People were able to buy shares with just a 10% deposit, and pay off the debt when they had sold their shares. This was called 'buying on the margin'.

### What were the positive effects of changes to shares in the 1920s?
The increased popularity of shares and speculation in the 1920s had a number of effects on the economy. Some of these were positive.
- ✓ People made huge profits from speculation, and therefore had more money to spend on goods.
- ✓ Businesses could use the money that they received for shares to increase production and expand.

### What were the negative effects of changes to shares in the 1920s?
The increased popularity of share and speculation in the 1920s had two key negative effects.
- ✓ Because they were buying shares on the margin, people regularly got into debt to the banks. They could only pay back the banks if share prices continued to rise.
- ✓ Because so many more people wanted to buy shares, share values went up because of demand, not because the company was doing well. Share values were much higher than the company was really worth.

---

**DID YOU KNOW?**

Speculation meant people could profit from buying - and selling - shares.

Typically, $100 invested in 1920 would be worth $325 in 1929.

# THE US GOVERNMENT IN THE 1920S

*'A return to normalcy.'*
*Warren Harding, 1920*

**What did the American government do in the 1920s?**

During the 1920s, the federal government in America was Republican. This meant that they aimed to help businesses, rather than individuals or society.

**What principles did the American government have in the 1920s?**

The ideas and principles of the Republican governments of America in the 1920s helped the economic boom.
- They believed in laissez-faire - to 'leave alone'. This was the idea the government should let the economy run without too much interference.
- They had a 'business-first' attitude, and didn't tell business owners how to run their factories or treat their workers.

**What actions did the American government take to help the boom in the 1920s?**

The Republican government in the 1920s followed policies that helped business and the economy to boom.
- They aimed for low taxes, which meant people had more to spend.
- They prevented trade unions from standing up for workers' rights, so they didn't cost the business owners more money.
- They charged high tariffs (taxes) on foreign goods to encourage people to 'buy American'.
- They allowed some businesses to become very big and dominant through huge corporations called trusts. For example, Carnegie (steel) and Rockefeller (oil) controlled most of their sectors of industry.

**Who were the presidents in the American government of 1920s?**

During the 1920s there were 3 presidents in America, all of whom were Republican.
- Warren Harding was president from 1921 until his death in 1923.
- Calvin Coolidge was president from 1923 to 1929.
- Herbert Hoover was president from 1929 until 1933.

---

### DID YOU KNOW?

**Some of the Republican presidents had interesting habits...**
Calvin Coolidge apparently used to play a practical joke on his staff by ringing the bells to summon them, and then hiding behind the curtains.

---

# DECLINING INDUSTRIES

*'Eleven cent cotton, forty cent meat, How in the world can a poor man eat?'*
*Lyrics from the folk song, 'Eleven Cent Cotton'*

**What was the decline in industries in 1920s America?**

Although many American industries boomed in the 1920s, others struggled because of the changes to the economy.

### Which industries declined in America during the 1920s?
A number of industries struggled in 1920s America:
- Shipbuilding.
- Coal mining.
- Railways.
- Farming.
- Textiles.

### How did the First World War cause some industries to decline in 1920s America?
The end of the First World War spelled trouble for some industries that had grown during it.
- When the war ended, there was no longer such a high demand for ships, and the shipbuilding industry went into decline.
- The end of the war led to a drop in demand and in the prices of food, so many farmers struggled. Many had gone into debt to expand their farms during the war, and couldn't pay it back.

### Which industries replaced those in decline in 1920s America?
Some industries in 1920s America went into decline because they were replaced by new goods and technology.
- The rise of the motor car and the building of roads meant less use of the railways.
- Cotton farmers and textile workers found that there was less demand for their goods as they had been replaced by new synthetic fabrics such as nylon and rayon.
- Less coal was needed as more homes and businesses were powered by electricity *(p.26)*, produced by hydro-electric dams.

### What social changes caused the decline of some industries in 1920s America?
Some industries were negatively affected by social changes in US society.
- Prohibition *(p.49)* (the ban on alcohol) affected farmers who produced hops, apples, grapes and barley, which were no longer needed to make alcoholic drinks.
- As women's fashions changed and skirts became shorter, there was less demand for cotton and textiles.

### What were the effects of declining industries in America in the 1920s?
When an industry went into decline, it meant that its workers suffered.
- Many found that their wages dropped.
- Workers either lost their jobs or found they were less stable, and experienced periods of unemployment.
- Strikes became more common and more violent.
- Because many areas were dominated by traditional industries, it was difficult for workers to find work in other sectors unless they moved away.
- Many of the workers in declining industries lacked the skills and training to find work in the new ones.

### What were the causes of decline in the shipbuilding industry in 1920s America?
Shipbuilding was one of the industries that didn't benefit from the boom. When the First World War ended, demand for ships dropped and shipbuilders struggled to find work.

### What were the causes of decline in the coal industry in 1920s America?
Many miners found their wages dropping as demand for coal dropped.

- ✅ The rise of electricity *(p.26)* from hydroelectric dams meant that homes and factories were no longer heated or powered by coal.
- ✅ Oil and gas also replaced coal as fuel in homes and factories, leading to overproduction in the coal industry.
- ✅ Better technology meant that coal could be burnt more efficiently, reducing the amount needed.
- ✅ The decline of the railways meant that less coal was needed to power steam engines.

 **What were the causes of decline in the railway industry in 1920s America?**

The use of the railways declined as more roads were built, and cars and lorries were used to carry passengers and freight instead of steam engines.

 **What were the causes of decline in the textiles industry in 1920s America?**

The textile industry went into decline in the 1920s for a number of reasons.
- ✅ New synthetic textiles such as rayon and nylon, made by the chemical industry, started to replace cotton.
- ✅ New fashions meant that skirts were shorter and less material was used for clothes, so demand for textiles fell.

 **What were the causes of decline in the farming industry in 1920s America?**

Agriculture in America suffered some of the most serious economic problems of the 1920s for a number of reasons.
- ✅ When the First World War ended, demobilisation meant that soldiers returned to their farms and demand for food from Europe fell. This meant that prices dropped, making life difficult for many farmers who had expanded their farms to meet the demand of the war years.
- ✅ Countries such as Canada and Argentina began to compete with the USA in the worldwide sale of grain.
- ✅ Prohibition *(p.49)* was introduced, which meant that the production of alcohol became illegal. This reduced the demand for barley, apples, hops and grapes, which were used to make alcoholic drinks.
- ✅ The consumer society meant that people's food tastes changed. They preferred more luxurious food than cereal.
- ✅ The demand for cotton fell with new fashions and synthetic textiles, so cotton farming went into decline.
- ✅ Many farmers had begun to use new production methods and machinery to grow more crops. This led to over-production and meant that food prices dropped.
- ✅ The US government *(p.15)* put tariffs on food imports from other countries. They retaliated by putting tariffs on American food, so it was harder for US farmers to sell their goods overseas.
- ✅ The use of machines, such as tractors, rather than horses meant that farmers had to buy fuel to keep their farms running.

### DID YOU KNOW?

**Not all industries - or people - benefitted from the boom.**
In 1928, female workers in coal mines earned just $9 for a 70-hour week.

# FARMING IN 1920S AMERICA

*'The farmer has to be an optimist or he wouldn't still be a farmer.'*
Will Rogers

 **How did farming change during the 1920s in America?**

Farming in 1920s America suffered serious problems of overproduction. Although farmers were producing more goods, there was less demand for them and so farmers' crop and produce prices fell.

**Why did farmers produce more in 1920s America?**

Farmers were able to produce 9% more produce in the 1920s, for a number of reasons.

- ☑ The Agricultural Credit *(p.24)* Act of 1923 made it easier for farmers to borrow money to modernise their farms.
- ☑ Mechanisation and the use of tractors meant that more food could be produced with fewer workers.
- ☑ During the war, new seeds, pesticides and fertilisers improved production.

 **Why did farmers stop selling so much food in America in the 1920s?**

During the 1920s, demand for agricultural produce fell, and as a result prices dropped.

- ☑ When the First World War ended, demand for food from Europe fell. This meant that prices dropped, making life difficult for many farmers who had expanded their farms to meet the demand of the war years.
- ☑ Prohibition *(p.49)* was introduced, which meant that the production of alcohol became illegal. This reduced the demand for barley, apples, hops and grapes, which were used to make alcoholic drinks.
- ☑ The demand for cotton fell with new fashions and synthetic textiles, so cotton farming went into decline.
- ☑ The US government *(p.15)* put tariffs on food imports from other countries. They retaliated by putting tariffs on American food, so it was harder for US farmers to sell their goods overseas.

 **What was the effect of the decline in American farming in the 1920s?**

The changes to farming in the 1920s led to a number of problems for farmers and farmworkers.

- ☑ Food prices dropped and farmers could no longer get as much money for their crops.
- ☑ Farmers lost money. About two-thirds of US farmers were running their farms at a loss.
- ☑ Many farmers went bankrupt and had to leave their farms.
- ☑ There were 1 million fewer jobs for farmworkers by the end of the 1920s.

> **DID YOU KNOW?**
>
> **American agriculture in the 1920s did not benefit from the economic boom.**
> Fewer than 10% of farmers had electric lights or running water supplies.

# THE ROARING TWENTIES

*'The parties were bigger. The pace was faster. The shows were broader. The buildings were higher, the morals were looser and the liquor was cheaper.'*
F Scott Fitzgerald

 **What were the Roaring Twenties?**

The 'Roaring Twenties' is the term often used to refer to the decade of the 1920s in America. The rapid economic growth and rise of prosperity and consumerism *(p.25)* occurred alongside rapid social change, which often resulted in increased tension.

> **DID YOU KNOW?**
>
> **Slang became more more popular in American culture in the 1920s.**
>
> 'Cheaters' were glasses, an 'egg' was a wealthy person, and an alcoholic drink was known as 'giggle water'.

# THE ROLE OF WOMEN IN 1920S AMERICA

*'The problem of women's freedom is how to arrange the world so that women can be human beings.'*
*Crystal Eastman, 1920.*

### How did the role of women change in America after the First World War?

The roles and rights of women in America changed in many ways during the years following the First World War, with some gaining more freedom.

### What happened to American women in the First World War?

The First World War gave women some opportunities but didn't remove all the barriers that they faced.

- Women were able to perform the jobs of men who went to fight and made up one fifth of the workforce.
- They were still expected to stop working if they got married.
- Most still worked in low-paid, low-status sales and secretarial roles.
- They could vote in local elections in some states.
- Most were expected to perform all of the domestic labour and to look after housework and the children.
- Drinking and smoking were seen as socially unacceptable for women.
- If they went out, they were expected to be accompanied by a chaperone to check their behaviour.

### How did American women work in the 1920s?

During the economic boom of the 1920s, more women were able to work.

- Two million women joined the workforce during the 1920s.
- Different types of jobs were available to women, but most worked in traditionally female roles such as secretaries.
- More married women worked, but this was still a small proportion. By 1929 only 12% were in the workforce.
- Women did not earn as much as men, even in a similar job.
- Women from ethnic minorities were usually given the lowest paid jobs. Many worked as servants.

### How did the political rights of American women change in the 1920s?

Women's political status changed after the First World War.

- In 1920, women were awarded the right to vote by the Nineteenth Amendment.
- Many women chose to vote for the same people as their husbands.
- By the end of the 1920s there were 145 women in state governments, but only two in the House of Representatives.

## What laws were made for women in 1920s America?
Because women could vote after 1920, more laws were introduced to help them by, for example, providing more health and maternity care.

 ## How did the social position of American women change in the 1920s?
Women's role, and ideas about what behaviour was acceptable, changed in the 1920s.
- ☑ More women got divorced.
- ☑ On average, women had fewer children.
- ☑ Most women were still expected to look after the home and children.
- ☑ Many consumer goods were household appliances, which made housework easier and gave women more leisure time.
- ☑ Some women became flappers.

> **DID YOU KNOW?**
> 
> **Increasing freedom for women caused social change.**
> In 1914, there were 100,000 divorcees; this had doubled by the 1930s.

# FLAPPERS
*'...lovely, expensive and about nineteen.'*
F Scott Fitzgerald, describing flappers

## What was a flapper?
Some women in 1920s America began to challenge the old ideas about women. They became known as flappers.

## Who were flappers?
Flappers were influential, but they only represented a small proportion of American women.
- ☑ They were usually quite young.
- ☑ They were usually unmarried.
- ☑ They were more likely to come from wealthier parts of society and be middle or upper class.
- ☑ They were unlikely to be from ethnic or racial minorities.

 ## What did flappers look like?
Flappers changed their appearance to challenge ideas about women and to look modern and free.
- ☑ They cut their hair short and sometimes coloured it.
- ☑ They wore bright makeup.
- ☑ They wore shorter skirts.
- ☑ They rolled their stockings down to the knee.
- ☑ They aimed for a slender, 'boyish' figure.
- ☑ Film star Clara Bow became a role model for flappers. She was known as the 'It Girl'.

### How did flappers behave?

Flappers challenged behavioural norms for women at the time.

- They went out unaccompanied to nightclubs, dances and parties.
- They drank and smoked in public.
- They danced in a way that was seen at the time as quite risque and sexual.

### What were the effects of flappers on American women in the 1920s?

Flappers challenged traditional attitudes, and so changed ideas about women at the time.

- Women became more independent and could go out without a chaperone.
- Women were able to make more obvious changes to their appearance.
- More women had sex before marriage.

---

**DID YOU KNOW?**

**As consumers, women were more able to influence production.**
Ford cars apparently introduced a variety of colours to please female consumers.

---

# ENTERTAINMENT IN 1920S AMERICA

*'A day without laughter is a day wasted.'*
Charlie Chaplin

### What role did entertainment play in 1920s America?

In 1920s America, for the first time, large numbers of ordinary people had the money and the free time to spend on entertainment and leisure activities. This led to the growth of the entertainment industry.

### Why did the entertainment industry grow in 1920s America?

In the 1920s Americans had higher wages but fewer working hours. This gave them more time and money to spend on leisure activities.

### What did people do for entertainment in the 1920s America?

There were a number of new and growing forms of entertainment in the Roaring Twenties.

- People went to the cinema.
- They listened to the radio.
- They went to sports events.
- They were more likely to travel on holiday or day trips.

---

**DID YOU KNOW?**

'King Kong' cost $650,000 to make in 1933, but made a profit of $4 million.

# CINEMA IN 1920S AMERICA

*'Adding sound to movies would be like putting lipstick on the Venus de Milo.'*
Mary Pickford

## What was cinema like in the 1920s?

Americans in the 1920s didn't have television, but more and more of them enjoyed going to the cinema to watch films.

## How did cinema develop in 1920s America?

There were 7 key developments in cinema in 1920s America:

- From 1922 some films were produced in Technicolor.
- Before 1927 films were silent, but then the first 'talkie' appeared. It was 'The Jazz Singer' starring Al Jolson.
- The first animated film, Disney's 'Steamboat Willie', appeared in 1928 and was followed by more cartoons.
- Hollywood in California, where the film industry was based, became a byword for glamour. People idolised film actors such as Rudolph Valentino and bought movie magazines to find out more about the stars.
- The film industry made about $2 billion a year from ticket sales.
- Films were often used to portray the 'ideal' lifestyle, and to advertise consumer goods and products.
- In 1930, the Hays Code introduced strict rules about the sort of morals that could be shown in films, as people were worried that films were corrupting society.

### DID YOU KNOW?

**Improved technology affected the film industry.**
The introduction of 'talkie' movies after 1927 saw the popularity of many famous stars - such as Clara Bow - drop, as their voices were not suited to film.

# SPORT IN 1920S AMERICA

*'If it wasn't for baseball, I'd be in either the penitentiary or the cemetery.'*
Babe Ruth

## What was sport like in 1920s America?

Many Americans spent their leisure time watching a variety of sports, and sports players became national celebrities.

## Who were sports stars in 1920s America?

There were a number of key stars in 1920s sport:

- Baseball players Babe Ruth and Lou Gehrig.
- Boxer Jack Dempsey.
- Golfer Bobby Jones.
- Swimmer Gertrude Ederle.
- Tennis champion Bill Tilden.
- American footballer Red Grange, known as the 'Galloping Ghost'.

> **DID YOU KNOW?**
>
> **American sports stars became celebrities in the 1920s.**
> When 1920s baseball favourite Lou Gehrig died of motor neurone disease in 1941, the illness became known as 'Lou Gehrig's disease'.

# JAZZ IN 1920S AMERICA

*'If you have to ask what jazz is, you'll never know.'*
Louis Armstrong

### What was jazz?
Jazz, a style of music, became so popular that the 1920s were known as 'the Jazz Age'.

### What influenced jazz music in 1920s America?
Jazz was American music that was influenced by the blues and ragtime styles of mostly black musicians.

### Who were famous jazz musicians in 1920s America?
Some jazz musicians became celebrities, such as Duke Ellington and Louis Armstrong.

### What dances did jazz inspire in 1920s America?
Jazz music inspired new dances such as the Charleston and the Black Bottom. Some Americans saw these as very immoral.

### What movie showed jazz music in 1920s America?
The first 'talkie' movie was called 'The Jazz Singer'. It was about a white man, played by Al Johnson, who disguised himself as a black one.

> **DID YOU KNOW?**
>
> **Jazz was the exciting new music of the modern age.**
> Famous jazz dances of the 1920s included the Charleston and the Black Bottom. They scandalised the older generation as they were seen as sexually suggestive.

# RADIO IN 1920S AMERICA

*'Radio broadcasting is spectacular and amusing, but virtually useless.'*
*E E Free, 1926*

 ### What happened with radio in 1920s America?
There were hundreds of radio stations at first. However, after the mid-1920s, big corporations such as the National Broadcasting Corporation (NBC) owned multiple channels which meant people across America were listening to similar shows and presenters.

### What radio stations were there in 1920s America?
Radios were used to broadcast everything from concerts and sermons to "Red Menace" ideas. The radio was certainly one of the most important inventions of the 1920s, because it not only brought the nation together, but it brought a whole new way for people to communicate and interact.

 ### What was on the radio in 1920s America?
There was live music, comedies, sports events and plays.

 ### Were there adverts on the radio in 1920s America?
Radio was also used to sell products, so many Americans spent a lot of time listening to advertisements.

 ### What dramas were on the radio in 1920s America?
Long-running dramas were broadcast in episodes and sponsored by soap manufacturers. These became known as 'soap operas'.

> **DID YOU KNOW?**
>
> **Radios were powered by electricity, and fuelled advertising and consumerism.**
>
> The first musical advertising jingle was introduced on the radio in 1926. It was for Wheaties cereal.

# TRAVEL IN 1920S AMERICA

*'Does mother sigh for a rest from daily routines? Take her auto-touring.'*

 ### Did people travel for leisure in 1920s America?
With 23 million cars on the road by 1929, travel became a national pastime for many Americans. They visited national parks, beauty spots, sports events, shopping centres and cities.

 ### What was the impact of travel in 1920s America?
The increased popularity of travel and tourism in 1920s America boosted businesses such as:

- ☑ Roadside cafes.
- ☑ Petrol stations.
- ☑ Motels.

**DID YOU KNOW?**

The rise of the motor car opened up the horizon.
400,000 km of roads were built in America during the 1920s.

# IMMIGRATION IN 1920S AMERICA

*'As soon as they step off the ships... our problem has only begun.'*
*Republican Senator James Heflin*

### How many people emigrated to America after the First World War?
More than 14 million immigrants moved to the USA from other countries between 1900 and 1920.

### Who were the White Anglo-Saxon Protestant immigrants in America in the 1920s?
Most of the earlier immigrants to the USA were white, Anglo-Saxon and Protestant. They were known as WASPs.
- They were from northern and western Europe.
- They were the largest ethnic group in the USA.

### Who emigrated to America in the 1920s?
Many immigrants to the USA after the war were from southern and eastern Europe. This meant that they differed from the WASPs in a number of ways.
- Many were Jewish or Catholic.
- They were poor.
- Many could not speak English, and were illiterate.
- They came from countries where there were strong beliefs in new and radical political ideas, such as communism or anarchism.

### Why were Americans worried about immigrants in the 1920s?
Many WASPs were worried about the new immigrants for several reasons.
- People were worried that they would accept lower wages and take their jobs away.
- They were a different religion and had different cultures.
- They were seen as bringing dangerous and radical political ideas. After the Russian Revolution of 1917 many were seen as communist.
- They were often poor and illiterate. People worried that they would take more from society than they would contribute.

### What were Henry Laughlin's views on immigrants in the 1920s?
Henry Laughlin was a influential sociologist who had racist ideas about the new immigrants in 1920s America.
- He believed that people from southern and eastern Europe were racially inferior.
- He suggested that the new immigrants were more likely to end up in prison or mental hospitals.
- He suggested that these new immigrants should be sterilised to prevent them from having children. Some states carried this out on a few people.

- His research on European countries in 1923 was used by Congress to inform new immigration laws.

## What laws were made about immigration in 1920s America?
In the 1920s, two new laws were bought in to reduce the number of new immigrants into America.
- The Emergency Quota Act of 1921.
- The National Origins Act of 1924.

## What was the effect of the Emergency Quota Act of 1921 on immigration?
The Emergency Quota Act of 1921 was designed to limit the number of immigrants, particularly those from southern and eastern European countries.
- It limited the total number of immigrants to 357,000 every year.
- It only allowed each country to send 3% of the number of people from that same country who were already living in the USA in 1920.
- It meant that more people could come from northern European countries that already had large populations in America. These were likely to be WASPs.
- It limited the number of immigrants from countries with a very different culture.

## What was the effect of the National Origins Act of 1924 on immigration?
The National Origins Act of 1924 restricted immigration even more than the Emergency Quota Act had done.
- It reduced the total number of immigrants allowed from 357,000 to 164,000.
- The percentage of immigrants from each country was reduced to 2% of the number of people from that same country already in the USA by 1890, rather than using the 1920 figures.
- It meant even fewer immigrants could come from southern and eastern European countries.

## What were the results of US immigration laws in the 1920s?
The new immigration laws of the 1920s had several results.
- Immigration fell from 1.4 million in 1914 to below 300,000 in 1929.
- New border patrols were set up in 1925 to prevent illegal immigrants.
- New ways of enforcing immigration laws were introduced.
- America stopped being an 'open-door country'.

### DID YOU KNOW?
**Some immigrants were seen as more desirable than others.**
Between 1900 and 1920, 12.5 million Europeans from desirable 'WASP' countries emigrated to the USA.

# THE RED SCARE OF THE 1920S

*'The blaze of revolution is eating its way into the homes of the American workman...'*
US Attorney General Mitchell Palmer, 1920

### What was the first Red Scare?

The first Red Scare took place after the First World War, as Americans became worried about the new immigrants, particularly those from eastern Europe.

### Who were people afraid of in the first Red Scare?

Americans were afraid of people who held radical political ideas.
- Communists, who believed that property should be taken from private owners and controlled by the state.
- Anarchists, who believed that the government should be abolished.
- People with extreme left-wing ideas, who often wanted to see massive change to society, brought about by violence.

### Why did people get scared in the first Red Scare?

In the 1920s, a number of events highlighted people's fear of new radical political ideas.
- Many new immigrants were coming from countries where radical ideas had taken hold, such as Russia.
- After the First World War, there was a lot of industrial unrest and strikes. These were a problem for politicians and business owners, and sometimes led to violence.
- In April 1919, 40 mail bombs were sent to the homes of important politicians.
- In June 1919, 8 cities were hit with bomb attacks.

### Who was Alexander Palmer in the first Red Scare?

Alexander Palmer was the Attorney General whose house was damaged by a bomb in June 1919. He reacted by trying to get rid of the radical political threat.

### How did the government react to the first Red Scare?

The American government *(p.15)*, led by Attorney General Palmer, began to hunt down people it believed were political radicals, using different methods.
- In 1919, Palmer set up the General Intelligence Board to spy on radical groups.
- It raided radical political groups, searching their offices and making arrests between November 1919 and 1920.
- On the 2nd January, 1920, raids took place in 33 different cities.

### What were the Palmer Raids during the first Red Scare?

The Palmer Raids took place at the end of 1919 and the beginning of 1920, when police and the General Intelligence Board arrested suspected political radicals and searched their offices.

### What was the General Intelligence Board in the first Red Scare?

The General Intelligence Board was a government policing group.
- It was set up by Alexander Palmer in 1919.
- It was set up to find out information about radical political groups.
- It was led by J Edgar Hoover.
- It later became the Federal Bureau of Investigation - the FBI.

## What were the effects of the first Red Scare?

The first Red Scare and the Palmer Raids had a number of effects on American society.
- Thousands of people were arrested.
- Around 600 people were deported.
- Some people died or committed suicide in the poor conditions in jail.
- Immigrants and immigration were blamed for political radicalism.
- There was more public support for the government to limit immigration.
- There was less public support for the trade unions and strikes, because they were seen as communist.
- The attitudes it created played a role in the Sacco-Vanzetti case (p.41).

### DID YOU KNOW?

**Many Americans feared the new radical political ideas.**
In 1901, an anarchist shot dead American President William McKinley.

# THE SACCO-VANZETTI TRIAL

*'Why were these men held as murderers and highwaymen?'*
John Dos Passos

## What was the Sacco-Vanzetti case?

The Sacco-Vanzetti case was a famous controversy in 1920s America that highlighted the institutional racism that existed in the justice system of the time.

## What crime was committed in the Sacco-Vanzetti case?

In Massachusetts in April 1920, two Italians committed an armed robbery in a shoe factory. They stole over $15,000, shot two people and escaped.

## Who were Sacco and Vanzetti?

Sacco and Vanzetti were the two men who were arrested and charged with the armed robbery in Massachusetts.
- Nicola Sacco was an Italian shoe factory worker.
- Bartolomeo Vanzetti was an Italian fish salesman.

## Why were Sacco and Vanzetti arrested?

Sacco and Vanzetti were arrested in May 1920.
- They tried to run from police and were armed with guns when they were arrested.
- Both men were found to be anarchists.
- Sacco and Vanzetti believed they had been arrested because of the Red Scare.
- They lied to police about their whereabouts, alibis and beliefs after their arrest.

### What was the evidence against Sacco and Vanzetti?
There were several pieces of evidence used to prosecute Sacco and Vanzetti in their trial, that were seen to prove their guilt.
- The bullet fired in the robbery could have been from Sacco's gun.
- Vanzetti had a previous conviction for armed robbery.
- Both men were anarchists and had avoided military service.
- There were 61 eye-witnesses who put them at the scene of the crime.

### What was the evidence for Sacco and Vanzetti?
There several pieces of evidence used at the Sacco-Vanzetti Trial that suggested they were innocent.
- 107 eye-witnesses said that they had been elsewhere at the time of the crime.
- Character witnesses testified that the men had a good reputation.
- The gun was tampered with in a later trial.

### What happened at the Sacco-Vanzetti trial?
It took a year to bring the case to trial, and many people weren't prepared to be jurors. However, a verdict was reached in less than 24 hours.

### What was the verdict in the Sacco-Vanzetti trial?
Sacco and Vanzetti were found guilty on 14th July 1921, and sentenced to death. They were eventually executed in 1927.

### Why was the verdict in the Sacco-Vanzetti trial seen as unfair?
The Sacco and Vanzetti verdict was seen as unfair for several reasons.
- The judge in the trial, Judge Thayer, was a well-known anti-anarchist.
- Many Americans were anti-anarchist and anti-immigration. This meant that the jury was likely to be biased against them.
- The evidence wasn't conclusive.

### What were the results of the Sacco-Vanzetti trial?
The Sacco-Vanzetti trial had far-reaching results.
- Sacco and Vanzetti were executed in 1927.
- There were protests in 60 countries around the world against the sentence.
- In 1921 a mail-bomb was sent to the American Embassy in Paris in protest.
- The Sacco-Vanzetti Defence Committee raised over $300,000 to help them.
- A 'Sacco and Vanzetti Memorial Day' was introduced in Massachusetts in 1977, and a proclamation declared that their trial had not been fair.
- The controversy over their guilt or innocence continues to this day.

---

**DID YOU KNOW?**

During the First World War, Sacco and Vanzetti fled to Mexico to avoid conscription into the army.

# THE EXPERIENCE OF BLACK PEOPLE IN 1920S AMERICA

*'The cost of liberty is less than the price of oppression.'*
W E B Dubois

### What was the experience of African Americans in the USA in the 1920s?

Although slavery had ended in America in 1865 and 400,000 African Americans had served in the First World War, many continued to experience racial discrimination after 1918.

### How were African Americans treated in the southern states in the 1920s?

Many African Americans had been slaves in the southern states of America, and still experienced racism at the end of the First World War.

- The Jim Crow laws had been introduced to segregate African Americans from white people. They couldn't use the same cinemas, schools or bathrooms and had to sit in different sections on buses.
- Education was less accessible for African Americans. Only about 1% of those in the south could attend high school.
- The Supreme Court refused to challenge the Jim Crow laws.
- Many African American men accused of a crime were murdered by lynch mobs.
- They had little protection from the government or police.

### How did the Jim Crow laws affect African Americans in the 1920s?

The Jim Crow laws were introduced in a number of southern states to keep African Americans separate from white people, and were still in force after the First World War.

- African Americans couldn't attend the same schools or even use the same books as white people.
- They had to use different parts of restaurants and different bathrooms.
- They were segregated on transport, using separate railway carriages, standing on particular sections of railway platforms, and sitting at the back of the bus.
- African Americans had to use separate cinemas and entrances to shops and buildings.

### What was the experience of African Americans in the north of the USA in the 1920s?

Black people in the northern states of America suffered less institutional racism, but still experienced discrimination and prejudice.

- Beginning in the First World War, about 1.5 million African Americans moved from the south of America to the north in what was known as the Great Migration.
- Many could only find low-paid, unskilled, low-status work.
- Their low earnings meant they tended to live grouped together in areas of poor housing called ghettos, still segregated because of their pay. These ghettos included Harlem in New York.
- There were race riots after the First World War because of the resentment caused by competition over jobs. The number of returning ex-soldiers, and the decline of older industries, meant many white people felt threatened by the influx of African American workers.

### What were the effects of racism on African Americans in the 1920s?

The discrimination inherent in American society after the First World War affected African Americans in a variety of way.

- Fewer educational opportunities meant that black people were less able to get well-paid, skilled jobs. Many had to work as domestic servants, farmworkers or unskilled factory workers.
- African Americans had less job security and were more likely to lose their jobs in times of economic hardship.
- The standard of living was lower, partly because of segregation policies and partly because earnings were lower.

- Black people had fewer voting rights, as some white people tried to stop them voting, and they were forced to take literacy tests to vote in the south.

### What organisation were set up by African Americans in the 1920s?

During the 1920s, several organisations that had been founded to promote the cause of African Americans grew and thrived.
- The NAACP (National Association for the Advancement of Colored People), founded by W E B Dubois, grew to over 90,000 members.
- The UNIA (Universal Negro Improvement Association), founded by Marcus Garvey, supported African Americans in starting their own businesses and had more than one million members in the 1920s.

### Were there any improvements for African Americans in the 1920s?

Life in the 1920s saw some small improvements for some African Americans:
- There were some universities in the north, such as Howard College, where black people could get a higher education.
- The rise of jazz turned some black people into world-famous celebrities. Actors such as Paul Robeson also gained international fame.
- African American culture thrived in Harlem, in New York, leading to a rise in African American art and poetry.
- There was a growing black middle class in Chicago and New York. This remained small, but fought for more rights for African Americans.

**DID YOU KNOW?**

In 1930, the average life expectancy was 48 years old for black people, but 59 years old for white.

# THE KU KLUX KLAN IN THE 1920S

*'Literally half the town belonged to the Klan when I was a boy.'*
Robert Coughlan

### What was the Ku Klux Klan?

The Ku Klux Klan, or KKK, was a white supremacist organisation that aimed to ensure white people continued to have more rights than, and power over, other races. Its members dressed in white robes and hoods.

### What was the history of the Ku Klux Klan?

The Ku Klux Klan existed for many years before the First World War, but its power grew after the conflict.
- It was formed in the 1860s, after the American Civil War.
- Its actions were restricted by the government in 1871 through the Ku Klux Klan Act, but it continued as an underground movement.
- Insurance salesman William Simmonds restarted the organisation in 1915 after being inspired by the film, 'Birth Of A Nation'.
- At its height, in 1925, it had 5 million members.

### Who were the members of the Ku Klux Klan?
Most KKK members were white churchgoers from southern areas of America who were regarded as respected members of society.

### What did the Ku Klux Klan believe in?
The Ku Klux Klan expanded its beliefs after the First World War.
- They believed WASPs - White Anglo-Saxon Protestants - should fight for survival and dominance over other races.
- They believed immigration threatened WASPs and should be stopped.
- They enforced some traditional Christian values by attacking people of other religions and groups they saw as 'immoral', such as divorcees.
- They claimed segregation was supported by the words of the Bible.

### How was the Ku Klux Klan organised?
When William Simmonds set up the new KKK, he increased its appeal by making it more like an exclusive club with a mysterious code.
- The Klan was divided into chapters, or local groups, called Klaverns.
- There were different levels of authority in the Klan. Klaverns were led by Kleagles, who answered to Klugs. The overall leader was called the Imperial Wizard.
- The Klan's rules were written in a book called the Koran.

### What did the Ku Klux Klan do?
The KKK used several methods to intimidate and persecute anyone it felt was a threat to WASP supremacy, including black people, immigrants and critics.
- Its members intimidated people. Sometimes they would burn crosses outside their victims' homes to denote them as a target.
- The Klan used violence and members were often involved in lynchings. They also beat, burned, and tarred and feathered their victims.
- Its members protested against politicians with whom it disagreed and influenced lawmaking where possible.
- Members boycotted any businesses owned by those who disagreed with them.

### How did the Ku Klux Klan grow in the 1920s?
The Ku Klux Klan grew rapidly in the 1920s.
- Public relations experts Elizabeth Tyler and Edward Clarke helped Simmonds to make the Klan seem more appealing to people.
- Kleagles could keep $4 of the $10 joining fee, which meant that they encouraged more people to join.
- People might be intimidated or threatened if they refused to join or tried to leave.
- It was popular with the members of the middle classes who wanted to force their values onto others and felt threatened by the changes in society.

### Why did the Ku Klux Klan become so powerful in America in the 1920s?
By the mid-1920s, the Klan was very powerful.
- It had a lot of members. By 1923 there were 5 million members in 4,000 chapters, or Klaverns.
- It had some powerful members, including a few senators, a governor and a mayor.
- It contained judges and police officers, who could protect members who broke the law, or use the law to persecute people.

**Why did the Ku Klux Klan lose its influence?**

After 1925, the influence of the Klan began to fall.

- ☑ In 1925, a Grand Dragon (state) leader of the Ku Klux Klan, David Stephenson, was found guilty of the rape and murder of a young woman.
- ☑ The reputation of the Klan was damaged by the trial of David Stephenson, and people felt more confident about criticising it.
- ☑ Membership fell. By 1929 it only had 200,000 members.

### DID YOU KNOW?

In the early 1920s, there were around 50 lynchings a year.

# RELIGIOUS DIVIDES IN 1920S AMERICA.

*'The nation is Protestant and must remain so.'*
*Spokesperson for the Ku Klux Klan, 1924*

 **What was the religious divide in America in the 1920s?**

Although there were many religions in America in the 1920s, most people were Protestant. Some were fundamentalists, believing everything in the Bible literally. Others were modernist and incorporated science into their beliefs.

 **What beliefs led to the religious divide in 1920s America?**

Protestantism in the USA was divided according to people's beliefs:

- ☑ Fundamentalists believed that everything in the Bible was literally true.
- ☑ Modernists believed that parts of the Bible could be interpreted differently, and mixed their understanding of it with science.

 **What was the impact of this religious divide in 1920s America?**

Different religious beliefs had an impact on local laws and decisions by individual states about issues such as education. In Tennessee, for example, it was illegal to teach the theory of evolution in schools.

### DID YOU KNOW?

**On the first day of the Scopes Trial 1,000 people crowded into the courtroom.**

300 of them had to stand.

# AMERICAN FUNDAMENTALISM

*'The Bible states it; it must be so.'*
William J Bryan

### What was fundamentalism in America?
Some Christians in 1920s USA were fundamentalists. They were Protestants who believed the Bible was literal and should be followed very strictly.

### What did American fundamentalists believe?
Fundamentalists believed that everything in the Bible happened as it was written and should be taken literally. This included the creation story about how the earth was formed in seven days.

### Who were the fundamentalists in America?
Many Americans from all walks of life were fundamentalist Christians, but there were some broad patterns in terms of where they were in 1920s society.

- They often proclaimed that they had strict morals and traditional values.
- Although some lived in cities, they were more influential in rural areas and small towns.
- Many lived in the 'Bible Belt', an area that crossed through the southern and midwestern states of America.
- Some were very influential. For example, Aimee Semple McPherson used the radio to spread fundamentalist messages and built a huge church in Los Angeles.

> **DID YOU KNOW?**
> William J Bryan offered $100 to anyone willing to admit that they descended from an ape.

# AMERICAN RELIGIOUS MODERNISM

*'Scopes isn't on trial, civilization is on trial. No man's belief will be safe if they win.'*
Clarence Darrow

### Who were the modernists in 1920s America?
Some Christians in 1920s USA were modernists who did not take all of the Bible literally.

### What did modernists believe in the USA?
Religious modernists in 1920s America believed in Christianity, but didn't agree with the fundamentalist view.

- Modernists interpreted the Bible using modern scientific discoveries.
- They often still believed that God had created the world, but not in seven days, as described in the Bible.
- They accepted some of Charles Darwin's ideas about evolution.

# THE SCOPES TRIAL, 1925

*'Mr Bryan sprang to his feet, his face purple, and shook his fist... while he cried: 'To protect the word of God from the greatest atheist and agnostic in the United States.'*
*HL Mencken, Baltimore Evening Sun, 1925*

### What was the Scopes Trial?
The Scopes Trial (sometimes called 'the Monkey Trial') was an important trial in 1925 that highlighted the conflict between different American beliefs and attitudes.

### Who was the person on trial in the Scopes Trial?
Johnny Scopes was a modernist high school teacher who deliberately broke Tennessee law in 1925 by teaching evolution in school. He was famously put on trial, raising awareness of the controversy.

### What was the Scopes Trial about?
There were 4 main points to the Scopes Trial.
- ✅ The Scopes Trial was about the teaching of Charles Darwin's theory of evolution in schools.
- ✅ The Anti-Evolution League of America was set up to campaign against the teaching of evolution in schools, because it went against the fundamentalist interpretation of the biblical story of creation.
- ✅ In 1925, the state of Tennessee passed the Butler Act, which made it illegal to teach evolution in schools. Anyone who did so could be fined.
- ✅ A school teacher called Johnny Scopes, in Dayton, challenged the law and taught lessons on evolution.

### Who argued for fundamentalists in the Scopes Trial?
The prosecution in Scopes Trial aimed to support the fundamentalist point of view by finding him guilty.
- ✅ Scopes was prosecuted by the famous fundamentalist lawyer, William Jennings Bryan.
- ✅ The prosecution proved that Scopes had taught evolution,
- ✅ The prosecution attacked the defence's attitude to the Bible.
- ✅ The prosecution defended the fundamentalist view.

### Who argued for modernists in the Scopes Trial?
Scopes was defended by the famous lawyer, Clarence Darrow, an agnostic. He turned the trial into a discussion about fundamentalism, put William Jennings Bryan on the stand and called his fundamentalist beliefs foolish.

### What was the verdict in the Scopes Trial?
Although Darrow tried to turn the trial into a discussion about creationism and evolutionism, the judge insisted that it was about whether Scopes had broken the law by teaching evolution. He had, and was fined $100.

### What were the effects of the Scopes Trial?
The Scopes Trial had a number of results.
- ✅ In the short term, the trial seemed to have little effect.
- ✅ The Butler Act remained in place until 1967.
- ✅ The Anti-Evolution League of America persuaded more states to ban the teaching of evolution.
- ✅ However, the modernists had succeeded in challenging fundamentalist control.
- ✅ The trial was reported nationwide and raised awareness of the debate.
- ✅ Bryan's fundamentalist views were undermined. Many people mocked them.
- ✅ The trial highlighted the divide between fundamentalist, rural America and modernist, urban society.

> **DID YOU KNOW?**
> Prosecutor William J Bryan collapsed and died five days after the Scopes Trial.

# PROHIBITION

*'Prohibition makes you want to cry into your beer, and denies you the beer to cry into.'*
Don Marquis

## What was Prohibition?

In 1919, the Eighteenth Amendment made it illegal to make, sell or transport alcohol. This became known as Prohibition.

## Why was Prohibition introduced?

Since the 19th century, there had been a movement campaigning for a ban on alcohol.

- The Women's Christian Temperance Movement was set up in 1873 and the Anti-Saloon League in 1893. They used peaceful methods to campaign against alcohol.
- They argued that it caused social problems such as unemployment, poverty and family breakdown.
- They suggested that it was bad for the economy because it meant that workers were less able.
- Religious groups claimed that drinking led to sin.
- It caused problems during the war because grain was needed for bread, not beer, and workers needed to be efficient. Later in the war, it was seen as unpatriotic because beer was traditionally German.
- Some historians have suggested that Prohibition was really about WASPs suppressing the habits and culture of newer immigrants.

## What were the benefits of Prohibition?

Prohibition had some benefits.

- It was relatively popular. A surprisingly large percentage - 40% - of Americans supported it.
- It led to a reduction in alcohol consumption.
- The health of some Americans improved, and incidences of illness such as liver disease dropped.
- Some Prohibition agents were very effective at seizing alcohol and enforcing the law. Moe Smith and Izzy Einstein were well known for this reason.

## What were the economic effects of Prohibition?

Prohibition caused a number of economic problems.

- The government lost income from the tax on alcohol.
- Farmers had less of a market for crops used to make alcohol, such as apples, grapes, barley and hops.
- Breweries and saloons were closed down.
- Thousands of Americans lost their jobs, and had less money to spend on goods and services.

## What problems did Prohibition cause for the police?

Prohibition caused massive problems in law enforcement. It became very difficult to make sure that people followed the law, and to stop the ones who broke it.

- Five states refused to enforce Prohibition.
- The Treasury Department only gave $2 million to enforce Prohibition across the whole country. This was not enough.
- Prohibition agents were poorly paid, which made them vulnerable to corruption and bribes.
- American juries refused to convict people who broke Prohibition laws.
- Many people disagreed with Prohibition and so were prepared to become law-breakers.

### What crimes did Prohibition cause?

Prohibition made it illegal to make, transport and sell alcohol, but many people were prepared to break these laws.

- People who made alcohol illegally were known as moonshiners, and the drinks they made were given names such as moonshine and bathtub gin. These were sometimes poisonous, causing serious illness, blindness and even death.
- People who transported and smuggled alcohol were known as bootleggers, because they would sometimes hide bottles of alcohol down their trouser leg. Some bootleggers smuggled millions of dollars worth of alcohol.
- People who sold alcohol illegally did so in secret drinking dens called 'speakeasies'.

### How did Prohibition lead to the rise of gangs?

Prohibition provided lots of opportunities for criminals to gain power and wealth, particularly in large cities such as New York and Chicago. They often worked together in large groups called gangs and were known as 'gangsters'.

### What crimes did Prohibition lead to?

With so much power and influence gangs were able to operate on a large scale. They committed more crimes as they grew to protect their empires.

- They used violence against rival gangs to protect their business.
- They controlled some politicians.
- They ran gambling dens and brothels.
- They ran protection rackets, taking money from businesses to 'prevent' damage to their property.
- They operated as loan sharks.
- They bribed Prohibition agents and policemen.
- They recruited ordinary citizens to help them make and transport alcohol.

### What were the effects of Prohibition?

By the 1930s, Prohibition had some unexpected results.

- By 1929, alcohol consumption was back to 70% of its 1914 level, despite being illegal to make, sell or transport.
- The Association Against the Prohibition Amendment was formed to bring an end to Prohibition.
- In 1933, the ban on alcohol was lifted and it could be legally sold again.

---

**DID YOU KNOW?**

**In 1929 there were 400 gang-related killings in Chicago alone.**
The Mayor, 'Big Bill' Thompson, was known to be a friend of Al Capone.

# AL CAPONE

*'You can get much farther with a smile, a kind word and a gun than you can with a smile and a kind word.'*
Al Capone (attributed)

### Who was Al Capone during Prohibition?
Al Capone became the most famous gangster of the Prohibition *(p.49)* era.

### What was Al Capone's background?
Al Capone's origins were similar to those of many gangsters in the Prohibition *(p.49)* era.
- Al Capone was based in Chicago.
- He originally worked for a crime boss called Johnny Torrio, and inherited control of the gang when Torrio retired.

### What were Al Capone's methods?
Capone was ruthless and aggressive, and used extreme measures to protect his business from other gangsters who wanted to profit from it.

### What did Al Capone do?
Capone was famous for both his success and his brutality.
- On 14th February 1929, Capone's gang killed seven members of a rival gang led by Bugs Moran. This became known as the Valentine's Day Massacre.
- As head of his gang, Capone earned up to $105 million a year from crime.

### How was Al Capone stopped?
Al Capone was eventually arrested and sentenced to 11 years in prison in 1931.
- Federal Agent Eliot Ness and his team of 'Untouchables' tried to stop Capone by raiding his bases and seizing alcohol. However, they were unable to stop or arrest him.
- Capone was eventually arrested for tax evasion of $200,000. He was imprisoned in 1931.

---

**DID YOU KNOW?**

**Al Capone was known by some for his generosity.**
He gave large tips to ordinary working people, and spend $30,000 on a soup kitchen during the Depression.

# LONG-TERM WEAKNESS IN THE US ECONOMY DURING THE 1920S

*'We have more cars, more bathtubs, oil furnaces, silk stockings, bank accounts, than any other people on earth'*
President Herbert Hoover, 1929

### What were the long-term weaknesses in the US economy after the First World War?

By the end of the decade several problems in the economy were becoming apparent including speculation, poverty, overproduction and tariffs.

### Why was speculation a long-term weakness in the 1920s American economy?

Speculation was buying shares to sell for a profit, based on the belief that prices would carry on rising. This led to more demands for shares, which inflated their prices artificially.

### Why was poverty a long-term weakness in the 1920s American economy?

71% of Americans lived on low incomes in the 1920s, and didn't have the spending power to buy consumer goods. This began to lead to under-consumption, where not enough goods were bought.

### Why was overproduction a long-term weakness in the 1920s American economy?

Factories carried on making consumer goods even though the people who could afford them had already bought them. Sales fell and so did prices.

### Why were tariffs a long-term weakness in the 1920s American economy?

America put taxes, called tariffs, on imports from other countries to encourage Americans to buy US goods. Other countries retaliated by putting tariffs on US goods, making it hard to sell overseas.

### What were the signs of long-term weakness in the 1920s American economy?

In the late 1920s, some financial experts began to recognise the signs that an economic slow-down was on its way.

- ☑ Wage increases were slowing down.
- ☑ Fewer houses were built.
- ☑ The amount of stock in warehouses was starting to rise, showing that sales were slowing down.
- ☑ The number of car sales was dropping.

---

**DID YOU KNOW?**

**In 1920, there had been four million shareholders in America.**
By 1929 there were twenty million, out of a population of 120 million.

# THE WALL STREET CRASH

*'The most disastrous decline in the biggest and broadest stock market of history rocked the financial district yesterday...'*
New York Times, 1929

### What was the Wall Street Crash?
The Wall Street Crash was an event in 1929 when the value of shares in the stock market *(p.26)* suddenly plummeted. It led to huge problems in the American economy.

### When did the Wall Street Crash happen?
The Wall Street Crash happened between October and November 1929.

### What led to the Wall Street Crash?
The Wall Street Crash occurred when confidence in share *(p.26)* prices fell, leading to a huge fall in their value.
- Increasing demand for shares meant their prices rose rapidly, but this was based on over-confidence rather than on the value of the businesses themselves.
- Many speculators 'borrowed on the margin' to buy shares, getting into debt with banks and intending to pay it off with the profit that they made when they sold their shares.
- From about 1927 there were signs of an economic slowdown, such as slowly rising unemployment and over-stocking of warehouses because of overproduction.
- In mid-1929, some experienced investors began to worry that share *(p.26)* prices would fall. They sold their shares, and prices then began to drop.

### What happened during the Wall Street Crash?
There were three key events:
- Once shareholders realised their shares prices were dropping, they began to panic and sell them.
- Because of the fall in demand for shares, their prices dropped rapidly.
- Share *(p.26)* prices plummeted in October and November as more and more investors desperately tried to sell their shares before they lost any more money.

### What did the Wall Street Crash mean for the American economy?
By the time share *(p.26)* prices levelled out, they were worth only a third of their September value. $26 billion had disappeared from the American economy.

---

**DID YOU KNOW?**

**On 'Black Thursday' - 24th October 1929 - nearly 13 million shares were sold on the stock market.**

Normally, a busy day would see the Stock Exchange handle 4 to 5 million shares.

# EFFECTS OF THE WALL STREET CRASH

*'$100 will buy this car. Must have cash. Lost all on the stock market.'*
*Sign seen on a car after the Wall Street Crash*

### What were the effects of the Wall Street Crash on the American economy?
The Wall Street Crash *(p.53)* was disastrous for the American economy.

### What effect did the Wall Street Crash have on banks?
The Wall Street Crash *(p.53)* meant serious problems for American banks.
- ✓ Because banks were major investors and shareholders, the Wall Street Crash *(p.53)* caused them to lose a lot of money.
- ✓ Many people had borrowed money from the banks to buy shares and couldn't pay it back.
- ✓ Because of the panic, many people took their money out of the banks before it was lost.
- ✓ When everyone tried to take their money at once it was called a 'run on the bank', and the bank would then fail.
- ✓ Because they were short of money, banks had to recall loans and stopped lending money to businesses.

### What effect did the Wall Street Crash have on businesses?
The Wall Street Crash *(p.53)* had a knock-on effect on businesses.
- ✓ Because of the panic, and because people lost money, demand for goods dropped.
- ✓ Without loans from the banks, many businesses couldn't afford to keep running and had to close down.
- ✓ Many businesses had to invest less, cut production and reduce their workers' hours.

---

**DID YOU KNOW?**

**Rockefeller lost 80% of his wealth in the Wall Street Crash.**
However, he still had $40 million left!

---

# THE GREAT DEPRESSION

*'We are the first nation in the history of the world to go to the poorhouse in an automobile.'*
*Will Rogers, 1931*

### What was the Depression?
From 1929 onwards, the American economy fell into Depression - a time when businesses struggled to stay open, unemployment rose and poverty became a serious problem for millions of people.

### What is the cycle of depression in 1930s America?
From 1929, the US economy entered the cycle of Depression.
- ✓ With less money, people couldn't buy as many goods.
- ✓ As demands for goods dropped, factories had to cut back on production.
- ✓ When they cut production, factories reduced their workers' hours or put them out of work.
- ✓ With less employment, people had less money to spend on goods.

**Why did people have less money in the Depression in 1930s America?**
The Depression led to a huge reduction in income and loss of savings for many people.
- Between 1928 and 1933, average wages fell by 60%.
- By 1932 over 5,000 banks - 20% of all the banks in America - had failed. Nine million customers lost all their savings.

 **Why was there less demand for goods in the Depression in 1930s America?**
Americans couldn't afford to buy as many goods, but international trade dropped too as other countries were also hit by the Depression. By 1933, demand for goods was less than a third of its 1929 level.

 **Why was there less production in the Depression in 1930s America?**
Because of reduced demand and lack of credit *(p.24)* from the banks, businesses were forced to cut production and struggled to survive.
- Between 1928 and 1932, industrial and agricultural production levels fell by 40%.
- Between 1929 and 1933, over 100,000 businesses shut down completely. Many more laid workers off or cut their hours.

 **Why did people lose their jobs in the Depression in 1930s America?**
Jobs became far more difficult to find and keep due to businesses failing and reduced production. By 1933, nearly a quarter of all Americans were unemployed.

 **How serious was poverty in the Depression in 1930s America?**
The problems of the Depression meant that many Americans experienced serious poverty.
- In 1932 alone, a quarter of a million Americans lost their homes. Homeless people lived in shanty-towns called 'Hoovervilles' or travelled the country trying to find work.
- Without government help, many Americans were forced to rely on relief, and on charity or state-run soup kitchens for food. The queues outside these were called 'bread lines'.
- Some Americans suffered from serious malnutrition. In New York in 1932, 20,000 children had insufficient food and 45 people died in hospital of starvation.

 **What international problems did the Depression in 1930s America cause?**
America had been supplying a lot of money in loans to Europe since the First World War. Once these loans stopped because of the Depression, European economies struggled and they couldn't buy American goods.

> **DID YOU KNOW?**
>
> 4.5 million cars were sold in 1929 in America, but only 1 million in 1932.

# FARMING IN 1930S AMERICA

*'Farmers are just ready to do anything to get even with the situation...'*
A N Young, 1932

 **What happened in farming in 1930s America?**
The early 1930s were terrible years for American farmers, who had already faced difficulties in the 1920s.

### How did the Depression affect American farmers in the 1930s?
Because people had less money, they bought less food. Demand and food prices fell even further and farmers struggled to make ends meet.

### Why were American farmers affected by the dust bowl in the 1930s?
The situation for farmers was made even worse by the dust bowl.
- Farmers on the Great Plains had over-farmed their land in the 1920s, causing the soil to erode.
- Droughts in 1930 and 1931 made the problem even worse, turning the soil into dry, crumbly dust.
- The dust was picked up by strong winds which created dust storms, or 'black blizzards', where the dust was too thick to see through.

### Where in America were farmers most affected by the dust bowl in the 1930s?
The dust bowl spread across the American plains, but the name was used specifically for the 5 worst-hit states.
- Oklahoma.
- Colorado.
- New Mexico.
- Kansas.
- Texas.

### What were the effects of the dust bowl on American farmers in the 1930s?
The dust bowl impacted farmers' ability to earn a living.
- The dust bowl affected about 17 million farmers. Many were unable to grow crops on their land and they had to pack up and leave their homes.
- About one million farmers and farmworkers started to move around to states where they might find work, such as California. They became known as 'Okies' and suffered terrible living conditions.

---

**DID YOU KNOW?**

Wheat prices fell from $1.04 per bushel in 1929 to 38 cents per bushel in 1932.

---

# PRESIDENT HOOVER

*'I'm the only person of distinction to have a depression named after him.'*
*President Herbert Hoover*

### Who was President Hoover?
Herbert Hoover was the Republican president of the USA from 1929 to 1933, at the beginning of the Great Depression.

### What were Herbert Hoover's political beliefs?
Hoover's actions in the Depression were based on his beliefs about America.
- He believed in 'rugged individualism' - that people should be able to look after themselves without relying on the government for help.

- He believed that the federal government should be laissez-faire and avoid taking too much control over people's lives. Instead, it should encourage state governments and businesses to help the economy.

### How did Hoover try to help the banks?

Hoover tried to help the banks that were failing in the Depression in different ways.

- The National Credit *(p.24)* Corporation (NCC) encouraged businesses to help banks, but businesses were already struggling themselves and didn't want to take the risk.
- The Reconstruction Finance Committee (RFC) used $2 billion of government money to help the banks.

### How did Hoover help farmers?

Hoover introduced a number of measure to try and solve the problems in farming.

- The Agricultural Marketing Act 1929 gave farmers money to support their farms. However, it struggled to make a difference.
- The Smoot-Hawley Tariffs in 1930 put taxes on imports of foreign food so that people would buy American.
- The Federal Farm Loan Act provided $125 million for farm mortgages. However, farmers were often still unable to pay them off.

### How did Hoover try to help businesses?

The National Business Survey Conference was set up for businessmen to discuss solutions, and the RFC gave money to banks to help businesses.

### How did Hoover deal with unemployment?

Although Hoover didn't give money from the federal government for relief, he did introduce measures designed to help the poor.

- The President's Emergency Committee for Employment (PECE) and President's Organisation for Unemployment Relief (POUR) were set up to encourage donations to help the poor, but couldn't raise enough.
- The Reconstruction Finance Corporation (RFC) allowed the federal government to loan $300 million to states for poor relief. However, only $30 million was actually loaned.
- The federal government doubled spending on public works, such as the Hoover Dam, to create jobs. However, proportionately it still spent far less than state governments.

### What were Hoover's successes in dealing with the Depression?

Hoover took the first steps to resolving the Depression and his actions did make a difference. The economic crisis was so big that perhaps nobody could have found a solution.

### Why was Hoover unsuccessful?

Hoover's actions in the Depression were criticised for a number of reasons.

- His actions didn't go far enough. His solutions were too small to make a difference to America in the Depression.
- The federal government didn't do enough. Instead it tried to organise states, banks and businesses into taking action instead - and they often didn't.
- Some solutions just didn't work. The Smoot-Hawley Tariff, for example, caused other countries to put tariffs on American food and made it harder to sell abroad.
- Some of his measures, such as tax cuts, seemed to help the rich rather than the poor. By helping businesses and banks, he seemed to be ignoring ordinary people in the crisis.
- His government only advised and encouraged change, rather than forcing anyone to take action.
- He became bitterly unpopular. Hoovervilles were named after him, and his actions with the Bonus Army were seen as repressive and cruel.

> **DID YOU KNOW?**
>
> **Hoover was deeply unpopular during the Depression.**
> As well as Hoovervilles, his name was given to the cardboard used to cover the holes in shoes ('Hoover leather') and newspapers ('Hoover blankets'). 'Hoover flags' were turned-out, empty trouser pockets.

# THE BONUS ARMY MARCHERS

*'They... needed their bonus now; 1945 would be too late, only buy wreaths for their tombstones.'*
John Dos Passos, 1932

### What was the Bonus Army?
The Bonus Army march was a large protest during the Depression.

### Who was in the Bonus Army?
The Bonus Army marchers were a group of about 20,000 ex-First World War soldiers and their families. Many were unemployed and living in poverty.

### Why did the Bonus Army march?
When they served in the First World War, soldiers were promised a bonus of a few hundred dollars in 1945. However, in 1931 they protested to try and persuade the government to pay it early, as it was desperately needed.

### What did the Bonus Army do?
The Bonus Army marchers walked to Washington and set up camp on Capitol Hill, opposite Congress, and waited for the government's decision.

### What did the government do about the Bonus Army marchers?
The government's refusal to give in to the Bonus Army led to the situation escalating.

- Congress refused to give the bonus early, but did give $100,000 to pay for the marchers' journeys home. Many left, but 5,000 stayed and continued to protest for their bonuses.
- President Hoover gave the marchers a deadline to leave and, when they didn't meet it, sent the police in. Two of the protesters were shot and killed.
- Hoover then sent in the army with tear gas, tanks and cavalry. The camp was flattened, 100 people were injured and a child was killed.

### What were the results of the Bonus Army march?
The Bonus Army was defeated and they didn't get the bonuses, but Hoover's reputation was destroyed by the brutality that had been displayed.

> **DID YOU KNOW?**
>
> The Senate voted not to pay the Bonus Army marchers by 62 votes to 18.

# FRANKLIN DELANO ROOSEVELT

*'It was his genius that he could speak clearly in warm-hearted leadership for us in an American period of difficulty.'*
Josephus Daniels, 1947

### Who was Franklin Delano Roosevelt?
Franklin Delano Roosevelt, known as FDR, became president in 1933, with the biggest majority ever seen in a presidential election. He remained president until his death in 1945.

### What was Roosevelt's background?
Roosevelt was from a wealthy and privileged background and enjoyed early political success. However, at the age of 39, an attack of polio left him partially paralysed.

### How was Roosevelt elected?
In his 1932 election campaign, Roosevelt promised Americans 'a New Deal (p.60)' to solve the Depression and protect them from it. He received 23 million votes and won in 42 of 48 states.

### How did Roosevelt plan to deal with the Depression?
Roosevelt planned to achieve his New Deal (p.60) in a number of ways:

- ✓ To use radio broadcasts called 'fireside chats' to explain his policies and win support for them.
- ✓ To use the support he had in Congress to turn his ideas into law.
- ✓ To use federal money to fund jobs, kick-starting the cycle of prosperity (p.18) and economic recovery. This was called 'priming the pump'.
- ✓ To set up new federal government agencies to solve specific problems of the Depression.

> **DID YOU KNOW?**
>
> **FDR was left disabled by an attack of polio when he was 39 years old.**
>
> He disliked drawing attention to his symptoms, and was rarely photographed in a wheelchair or being helped out of a car.

# 1932 ELECTION

*'The country needs and demands bold, persistent experimentation.'*
President Franklin D Roosevelt, 1932

### Who won the 1932 election?
Franklin Roosevelt (p.59) won the 1932 election with his idea for 'A New Deal (p.60) for the American people'.

### Why did Roosevelt win the 1932 election?
There are 5 key reasons why Roosevelt (p.59) won:

- ✓ He promised a 'New Deal (p.60)' for everyone. He said the government would have a more active role in the economy to help overcome the Great Depression.
- ✓ Unlike Hoover, he ran a positive and energetic campaign. He could make up to 15 speeches a day.

- ✅ He had already helped the poor as Governor of New York when he set up the first state-run relief scheme.
- ✅ The Great Depression worsened during Hoover's presidency.
- ✅ Millions of people had to exist in 'Hoovervilles' which were shanty towns named after, and blamed on, Hoover.

### DID YOU KNOW?
There was a record turnout at the voting booths in 1932.
40 million Americans voted in the presidential election.

# FIRESIDE CHATS
*'It cannot misrepresent or misquote. It is far reaching and simultaneous in releasing messages...'*
FDR's press secretary on the power of radio

### What were 'fireside chats'?
Fireside chats were addresses that Roosevelt *(p.59)* made on the radio to the American people.

### How many fireside chats did Roosevelt broadcast?
Between 1933 and 1944, he addressed the nation with 30 radio broadcasts.

### Why were the fireside chats important?
They helped the American people feel closer to the president and he reassured them during times of uncertainty. They boosted his popularity.

### DID YOU KNOW?
Most Fireside Chats began with the words 'Good evening, friends' and ended with a rendition of the Star-Spangled Banner.

# THE NEW DEAL AND SECOND NEW DEAL
*'I pledge myself to a New Deal for the American people.'*
Roosevelt's pre-election speech, 1932

### What was the New Deal?
The New Deal was the name given by Roosevelt *(p.59)* to his plans for solving the Depression by providing the 'three Rs' - relief, recovery and reform.

### What did Roosevelt mean by relief in the New Deal?
Roosevelt *(p.59)* promised to provide relief in the form of federal money to directly help the unemployed or by providing them with short-term work.

### What did Roosevelt mean by recovery in the New Deal?
Roosevelt *(p.59)* promised that the New Deal would bring economic recovery, kickstarting the cycle of prosperity *(p.18)* and raising incomes.

### What did Roosevelt mean by reform in the New Deal?
Roosevelt *(p.59)* promised the New Deal would reform, or change, the law so people had security in times of trouble and banks and businesses were safer.

### What was 'pump-priming' under Roosevelt in the New Deal?
Pump-priming described Roosevelt's *(p.59)* belief that government money could be used to break the cycle of depression.
- The federal government would provide money for schemes that employed people.
- People would be able to spend their wages on goods.
- This would stimulate demand.
- More demand would lead to greater production.
- Businesses would employ more people to produce more goods, leading to more money.

### What happened in the First Hundred Days of the New Deal?
As soon as Roosevelt *(p.59)* was inaugurated in March 1933, he pushed a number of important laws through Congress to expand the role of the federal government and set up the so-called 'alphabet agencies'. This three-month period of change became known as the First Hundred Days.

### How did Roosevelt solve problems with the banks in the New Deal?
Since the Crash, people had stopped trusting the banks. One of Roosevelt's *(p.59)* first actions was to restore confidence in the banks and encourage people to deposit their money in them again.
- Under the Emergency Banking Act on 9th March 1933, all banks were closed for a four-day bank holiday.
- Government inspectors checked the banks to make sure that they were run properly and money could be safely deposited.
- When the banks reopened, people knew they were safe institutions.
- Roosevelt *(p.59)* passed a law to insure banks for $2,500 per customer. People now knew that they would get some money back if the bank failed.
- About 5% of banks were closed down as they were unsound, but confidence was restored in those that were left.

### What did the New Deal do for the banks in the long-term?
The Banking Act of 1935 gave the government more power to control the banks.

### Was the New Deal limited?
The New Deal was criticised by many and did have some clear limitations.
- It did not solve unemployment. There was always at least one in ten people unemployed throughout the 1930s.
- Women faced discrimination. Some of the National Recovery Administration (NRA) codes set wages for women lower than those for men.
- It continued to discriminate against African Americans. For example, some Civilian Conservation Corps (CCC) campsites were segregated.
- After his re-election in 1936, Roosevelt *(p.59)* became concerned about the cost of job creation schemes like the TVA. He cut down the amount of spending but unemployment rose to 3 million.
- The Supreme Court limited the New Deal with cases such as Schechter Poultry v. United States which struck down the National Industrial Recovery Act.

### What was the Second New Deal?

By 1935, under the New Deal, unemployment had fallen but remained high. In 1936 Roosevelt *(p.59)* created a second New Deal to implement further reform. This mainly affected:

- Work.
- Housing.
- Labour relations.
- Farmers.
- Social security.
- Banks.
- Electrification.

### Why did FDR set up the Second New Deal?

There were a number of reasons why FDR *(p.59)* set up the Second New Deal in 1936.

- The Supreme Court had declared a number of alphabet agencies unconstitutional and shut them down. They needed to be replaced.
- The election of Congress in 1934 had led to more politicians who wanted further reform.
- Roosevelt *(p.59)* won another election by promising more changes.

### What were the aims of the Second New Deal?

The Second New Deal expanded on the aims of the first.

- More work relief for the unemployed.
- Improve workers' rights.
- Helping the rural poor settle on their own land.
- Provide for the old and vulnerable.

### How did the Second New Deal provide work?

The Second New Deal gave more money to provide more relief work for the poor and unemployed.

- The Second New Deal set up the Works Progress Agency (WPA), which spent $11 billion on employing eight million American men and women from all ethnic and working backgrounds.
- The CCC and PWA received $4 billion to provide more relief work for the unemployed.

### What did the Second New Deal do about housing?

The Second New Deal aimed to solve the problem of housing and Hoovervilles.

- The Resettlement Administration was set up to help the rural poor.
- The Housing Act set up an agency to build new suburban towns and homes to replace shanty towns.

### How did the Second New Deal help workers?

The NRA was declared unconstitutional in 1935, so the Wagner Act was introduced in the Second New Deal to change the law around trade unions.

- Workers were legally entitled to join trade unions. Union membership had risen to nine million by 1940.
- One union could be chosen for all the workers in a workplace to join. This was called a closed shop.
- Businesses were no longer allowed to fire workers for joining a union or to set up their own company unions.
- A National Labour Relations Board (NLRB) was set up for the federal government to work with the unions.
- There were more strikes after the Wagner Act. Some of these became quite violent.

### How did Second New Deal help farmers?

Agricultural workers were hit especially hard by the Depression. Many families travelled the country looking for work and living in terrible conditions. The Second New Deal aimed to help.

- ☑ The Farm Security Administration (FSA) offered loans for poor farmworkers and sharecroppers to buy their own land and set up camps for migrant farmworkers.
- ☑ The first Agricultural Adjustment Act had been declared unconstitutional, but the second set up quotas to control farm production, using heavy taxes on goods that were sold above the quota.

 ### How did the New Deal help the vulnerable?

The Social Security Act was introduced in 1935 and offered support to vulnerable members of American society. It was part of the Second New Deal.

- ☑ Workers paid 1% of their income into a pension scheme, which was matched by tax payments from their employer.
- ☑ Unemployed workers could get 16 weeks of half-pay after losing their jobs. This came from a tax paid by businesses with more than eight employees.
- ☑ Federal funding also provided support for families with children, very poor old people and the disabled.

 ### How did the New Deal increase the use of electricity?

From 1935, the scheme to bring electricity *(p.26)* to remote and rural areas of the USA was extended. This was part of the Second New Deal.

- ☑ The Rural Electrification Administration (REA) took over electrification and gave loans to rural areas across the US.
- ☑ By 1941, 35% of farms had electricity *(p.26)*.
- ☑ Some electricity *(p.26)* companies tried to stop the REA by building 'spite lines' to prevent poor communities from obtaining permission to access electricity.

> **DID YOU KNOW?**
> The New Deal was sometimes nicknamed 'Alphabet Soup' because it introduced so many alphabet agencies.

# THE ALPHABET AGENCIES

*'Work Relief preserves a man's morale. It saves his skill.'*
Harry Hopkins

 ### What were the alphabet agencies?

Roosevelt *(p.59)* set up a number of federal government agencies to solve the problems of the Depression. As their names were often abbreviated to initials, they became known as the alphabet agencies.

 ### How did setting up the alphabet agencies help farms?

The New Deal *(p.60)* contained a number of measures designed to help farmers, stop overproduction and raise food prices.

- ☑ The Agricultural Adjustment Administration (AAA) paid farmers to produce fewer crops. This aimed to end overproduction and drive food prices back up.
- ☑ The Commodity Credit *(p.24)* Corporation paid farmers to store food in warehouses instead of selling it.

- ☑ The Farm Credit *(p.24)* Administration improved mortgages for about 20% of farms, meaning farmers could pay more easily and avoid repossession.

### How did the alphabet agencies provide relief?

The New Deal *(p.60)* contained a number of laws designed to provide help for the poor.

- ☑ The Federal Emergency Relief Act provided $3 billion of federal money to be given to states to help the unemployed.
- ☑ The Homeowners Refinancing Act extended mortgages so that people could pay over 20 years instead of five, and afford their mortgage payments.

### How did alphabet agencies provide work?

Roosevelt *(p.59)* believed that the federal government should give people employment, rather than just handouts.

- ☑ The Civilian Conservation Corps (CCC) was set up to give outdoor conservation work to half a million 17 to 23-year-olds. They lived in camps and were paid $30 a month, most of which was sent home to their families.
- ☑ The Public Works Administration involved $3.3 billion of federal money for public works schemes and for hiring skilled workers.
- ☑ To provide short-term relief and see the unemployed through winter, the Civil Works Administration was set up in 1933 under the Federal Emergency Relief Administration (FERA) to provide temporary work.

### How did alphabet agencies help industry?

The National Recovery Agency (NRA) was established to fix some of the problems that had developed during the Depression for workers in business.

- ☑ The NRA set up a scheme where business owners could pledge to follow guidelines on wages, working hours, workplace conditions and prices.
- ☑ Nobody was forced to join the NRA scheme, but doing so meant they could display the NRA's blue eagle logo and show they were helping to resolve the Depression.
- ☑ 2.3 million businesses joined the scheme.
- ☑ The NRA also gave workers the legal right to join a union and campaign for better working conditions. Union membership rose from 3.1 million to 3.9 million in 1939.

### Which alphabet agencies helped the southern states?

The Tennessee Valley Authority (TVA) was set up to solve the problems of poverty, underdevelopment and soil erosion in states along the Tennessee River. Federal control allowed it to achieve more than state governments could.

### Which alphabet agencies increased the use of electricity?

At the beginning of the 1930s, only 10% of farmers had electricity *(p.26)* because it was too expensive to run it to remote areas. Various agencies were set up to help.

- ☑ The TVA built hydroelectric dams on the Tennessee River which provided electricity *(p.26)* to the surrounding area.
- ☑ In 1935, the Electric Home and Farm Authority helped farmers to buy electrical equipment.

### What were Roosevelt's alphabet agencies called?

Alphabet agencies were so called because they had long names that were shortened to their initials. There were many:

- ☑ AAA - Agricultural Adjustment Administration.
- ☑ CCC - Civilian Conservation Corps.
- ☑ PWA - Public Works Administration.
- ☑ WPA - Works Progress Administration.
- ☑ CWA - Civil Works Administration.
- ☑ EBA - Emergency Banking Act.

- FERA - Federal Emergency Relief Administration.
- NRA - National Recovery Administration.
- NLRB - National Labour Relations Board.
- RA - Resettlement Administration.
- FHA - Federal Housing Administration.
- NLRA - Wagner Act (National Labour Relations Act).
- REA - Rural Electrification Administration.
- FSA - Farm Security Administration.
- SSB - Social Security Board.

### DID YOU KNOW?

The New Deal did offer some opportunities for women and minorities.

The National Youth Organisation was headed by Mary Bethune, a black woman.

# OPPOSITION TO THE NEW DEAL

*'The New Deal is nothing more or less than an effort to take away from the thrifty...and give it to others who have not earned it and never will earn it.'*
*A Republican opponent of the New Deal, 1935*

### What was the opposition to the New Deal?

From 1933 onwards Roosevelt *(p.59)* faced opposition to his New Deal *(p.60)* measures for a number of different reasons.

### How did the Supreme Court oppose the New Deal?

From 1933 the Supreme Court upheld appeals against some alphabet agencies and declared them unconstitutional.

- The Supreme Court was made up of judges chosen by the Republican presidents in the 1920s and they were more likely to disagree with Roosevelt's *(p.59)* ideas.
- It upheld a complaint by the Schechter Brothers in the 'Sick Chicken Case' against the NRA, declaring the NRA unconstitutional and effectively closing it down.
- It upheld a complaint in 1936 by a cotton processor against the AAA, saying the federal government was doing the work of the state government *(p.15)*.

### How did FDR challenge opposition from the Supreme Court on the New Deal?

Roosevelt *(p.59)* was angry about the Supreme Court's judgements against his alphabet agencies. He tried to find ways to counteract the court's hostility.

- In 1937, he asked Congress to allow him to add a new judge to the Supreme Court for every existing judge aged over 70.
- This would mean adding six of his own judges and was called court-packing.
- Congress didn't agree to FDR's *(p.59)* plan, but afterwards the Supreme Court stopped challenging the New Deal *(p.60)*. Gradually the old Republican judges retired or died and Roosevelt could replace them.
- Roosevelt *(p.59)* received a lot of criticism for his threat - some people felt it was disrespectful to the American system of government *(p.15)* and that he was acting like a dictator.

### Why did Republicans oppose the New Deal?

Republicans disagreed with the New Deal *(p.60)* for three main reasons.

- ✓ They were natural opponents of Roosevelt's *(p.59)* Democrat policies.
- ✓ They believed government should be laissez-faire and avoid interfering too much in the lives of citizens. The New Deal *(p.60)* made the federal government very powerful.
- ✓ They believed in reducing spending to avoid high taxes and loans. The New Deal *(p.60)* involved spending vast amounts of money.

### What did Republicans do to oppose the New Deal?

After 1938 there were more Republicans in Congress, which gave them the power to try and stop the New Deal *(p.60)*.

- ✓ They cut spending on relief programmes.
- ✓ They investigated the alphabet agencies and levelled accusations against some of them.
- ✓ Blocked proposed new measures, such as proposals for more public works schemes in 1939.

### Why did businessmen oppose the New Deal?

Although businesses had benefitted from the New Deal *(p.60)* because it gave people money to buy their goods, many businessmen turned against it.

- ✓ Many businessmen and factory owners resented being told how to run their businesses by agencies such as the NRA. They preferred a laissez-faire style of government.
- ✓ They didn't like the support that was given to trade unions by the NRA and the Wagner Act, because unions could challenge their businesses.
- ✓ They disliked paying increased taxes to fund government spending.

### Did the Liberty League oppose the New Deal?

The Liberty League was founded in 1934 by conservatives from both parties to protect the rights of businesses to make their own decisions. They campaigned and spoke against New Deal *(p.60)* measures and paid for appeals against it.

### Which individuals opposed the New Deal?

Radical opponents of the New Deal *(p.60)* criticised it because they didn't think it did enough for poor people or to make American society more equal. Four influential critics were:

- ✓ Huey Long, the governor of Louisiana.
- ✓ Father Charles Coughlin, a Roman Catholic priest and radio preacher.
- ✓ Dr Francis Townsend, a retired public health official.
- ✓ Upton Sinclair, the novelist.

---

**DID YOU KNOW?**

$6.6 billion was spent on the New Deal in 1936.

# HUEY LONG

*'The trouble is, Roosevelt hasn't taken all my ideas; just part of them. I'm about one hundred yards ahead of him.'*
Huey Long

### Who was Huey Long?

Huey Long was the governor of Louisiana who was critical opponent of Roosevelt's *(p.59)* New Deal *(p.60)*. Long planned to run in the 1936 presidential election. He might have won had he not been assassinated in 1935.

### Why did Huey Long oppose the New Deal?

Long was popular as governor of Louisiana because he taxed businesses heavily to pay for public schemes. He opposed the New Deal *(p.60)* for two reasons:

- He believed the New Deal *(p.60)* didn't do enough for the poor.
- He claimed the NRA was controlled by big business, that the AAA left poor farmers homeless and that Social Security failed as it kept the poor poor.

### What did Huey Long do about the New Deal?

He started the 'Share *(p.26)* Our Wealth' scheme in 1934 and use it to provide everyone with a yearly income of $2,500. About eight million Americans joined the Share Our Wealth clubs.

- He suggested limiting personal fortunes to a maximum of $3 million.
- He proposed preventing anyone from making more than $1 million a year.
- He suggested free washing machines and radios for all Americans.
- He wanted to provide everyone with a yearly income of $2,500.
- He suggested old-age pensions for everyone over 60.

### How popular was Huey Long?

Huey Long's ideas were popular. About 8 million Americans joined the 'Share *(p.26)* our Wealth' scheme.

> **DID YOU KNOW?**
> Long once punched an elderly governor who called him a liar.

# FATHER COUGHLIN

*'Our government still upholds one of the worst evils of decadent capitalism; namely, that production must be only at the profit for the owners, for the capitalists.'*
Father Coughlin, 1934

### Who was Father Coughlin?

Father Charles Coughlin was a Roman Catholic priest and a radio preacher who was a critic of Roosevelt's *(p.59)* New Deal *(p.60)*. He originally supported FDR, but later turned against him.

### Why did Father Coughlin oppose the deal?
Originally a supporter of the New Deal *(p.60)*, Coughlin turned against Roosevelt *(p.59)* when Roosevelt refused to nationalise the banking system and provide for the free coinage of silver.

### What did Father Coughlin do about it?
Coughlin used three methods to oppose the New Deal *(p.60)*:
- ☑ In 1934 he set up the National Union for Social Justice, calling for more reforms of banking and business, fairer taxes, and for the government to take over some industries (nationalisation).
- ☑ In 1936, with Townsend and Gerald Smith of the Share *(p.26)* Our Wealth scheme, Coughlin set up the National Union Party and promoted William Lemke for president in the 1936 election.
- ☑ Father Coughlin broadcast his views on a radio programme called 'The Golden Hour', which had 30 million listeners.

### What impact did Father Coughlin have?
The Second New Deal *(p.60)* answered many of Roosevelt's *(p.59)* critics by providing some of the things they asked for, and making it harder for them to oppose him. Coughlin's anti-Semitic views also caused him to lose support.

> **DID YOU KNOW?**
> **Charles Coughlin's radio show was hugely popular.**
> In 1932 he had a weekly audience of 30 to 45 million listeners.

# DOCTOR TOWNSEND

*'But what of the millions of people who through long years of thrift and saving have been providing their own security?'*
Francis Townsend

### Who was Doctor Townsend?
Dr Francis Townsend was a retired public health official who opposed Roosevelt's *(p.59)* New Deal *(p.60)*.

### What actions did Doctor Townsend take?
Doctor Francis Townsend founded Old Age Revolving Pensions Ltd, which suggested that over-60s were given $200 monthly, funded by a 2% sales tax. 20 million people signed a petition to support this.

# UPTON SINCLAIR

*'We plan a new cooperative system for the unemployed.'*
Upton Sinclair

### Who was Upton Sinclair?
Upton Sinclair was a novelist who was a radical opponent of Roosevelt's *(p.59)* New Deal *(p.60)*. He ran for governor in California, but was defeated.

## What did Upton Sinclair do about it?

Upton Sinclair wrote The Jungle, about poor conditions for workers and argued that empty factories and land should be given to the unemployed to use.

> **DID YOU KNOW?**
>
> Upton Sinclair wrote adventure stories and pulp fiction to pay for his tuition at Columbia University.

# THE SUCCESS OF THE NEW DEAL

*'This nation asks for action, and action now.'*
*Roosevelt's inauguration speech, March 1933*

## How successful was the New Deal?

The success of the New Deal *(p.60)* is open to interpretation. It achieved a great deal but its impact was limited in some ways and places.

## How successful was the New Deal in farming?

The New Deal *(p.60)* saw some successes in farming, but also some failures.

- Farmers were given $4 billion in direct relief and farm income had nearly doubled by 1939.
- However, farm income didn't return to 1920s levels and many farmers owed the government money through mortgages and loans.

## How successful was the New Deal in banking?

The RFC helped 6,000 banks reopen after the Emergency Banking Act of March 1933. However, 106 had to close even after receiving government help.

## How successful was the New Deal in businesses?

Most businesses that survived after 1933 were able to make a profit. However, there was a serious recession in 1937-38 and the older, declining industries continued to struggle.

## Was the New Deal a success for unemployment?

Unemployment fluctuated after 1933.

- Unemployment never reached the same high levels of 1933 after Roosevelt *(p.59)* became president.
- However, it didn't return to its 1929 levels until the Second World War broke out.
- It had fallen significantly by 1937.
- When New Deal *(p.60)* spending was cut in 1938, unemployment rose again.
- The outbreak of the Second World War in 1939, and America's entry to the conflict in 1941, was what finally solved unemployment, as it provided jobs in the army and in the manufacture of war goods.

## Why wasn't the New Deal a success in solving unemployment?

There are a number of reasons why the New Deal *(p.60)* may not have been able to tackle the long-term problem of unemployment in the USA.

- The home market didn't recover, as many Americans continued to live in poverty. This was especially true of rural areas, where prices didn't recover until the Second World War.
- Competition and tariffs from other countries limited US overseas sales. Many countries were also suffering from the effects of the Depression, and couldn't buy many goods.
- Modern methods of production in agriculture and industry meant that fewer workers were needed.
- The global business cycle meant that the whole world fell into a recession in 1937 and 1938. The actions of one country could not make a difference to this.
- In some industries, such as agriculture, it was necessary to reduce jobs in order to make farming more efficient. There were therefore some self-inflicted job-losses in America.

### How successful was the New Deal in achieving the 3 Rs?

Roosevelt (p.59) had aimed to achieve 'the 3 Rs' with his New Deal (p.60) - relief, reform and recovery.

- The New Deal (p.60) succeeded in reform by making banks safer, regulating the treatment of workers, introducing social security and improving living conditions. However, it didn't really close the gap between rich and poor.
- Although the New Deal (p.60) did help to reduce unemployment, the fact it rose again when spending was cut showed the economy still hadn't recovered. Unemployment didn't stop being a problem until the Second World War.
- The federal government provided billions of dollars of short-term relief through the New Deal (p.60). Roosevelt's (p.59) ongoing popularity showed how much this was appreciated by ordinary people, but it didn't solve all the problems of poverty.

### Was the New Deal a success for women?

Women were given specific work by the women's and professional divisions of the WPA, and mothers received grants from the Social Security Act. However, most employment provided under the New Deal (p.60) was for men.

### Was the New Deal a success for black people?

30% of black families received relief, but this was often lower than the relief given to white people. Some CCC camps were integrated, but the AAA and NRA forced many poor black farming tenants from their land.

### Was the New Deal a success for the Native Americans?

The Indian Reorganisation Act of 1934 gave 7.4 million of acres to land to Native Americans. However, many were still very poor, reliant on alphabet agencies and had no support when they closed.

### Was the New Deal a success for trade unions?

The passing of the Wagner Act had mixed results for workers' rights and trade unions in America.

- Trade union membership grew to more than seven million.
- More strikes resulted in improved conditions for workers.
- Pay and working conditions improved overall.
- Some employers disliked the Wagner Act, and used violence against strikers.

### How was the success of the New Deal affected by the Second World War?

The start of the Second World War signalled the end of the New Deal (p.60), as it boosted exports by 70% in the first three years and stimulated employment.

---

**DID YOU KNOW?**

**There were around 4,700 strikes in America during 1937.**
One, in Chicago, led to 10 strikers being shot and 90 wounded.

---

| 70      *Quizzes, amazing exam preparation tools and more at GCSEHistory.com*

# UNEMPLOYMENT FIGURES IN DEPRESSION AMERICA

*'[Roosevelt] understood that the suffering of the Depression had fallen with terrific impact upon the people least able to bear it.'*
Frances Perkins, 1947

### What were the unemployment figures during the Depression?
The unemployment rate - the number of people without jobs - rose during the early years of the Depression and then fluctuated after reaching its height in 1933. The New Deal *(p.60)* eased, but didn't solve, the problem.

### What was the percentage of unemployment in the USA in 1929 before the Depression?
In 1929, before the Depression, 3.2% of the total workforce was unemployed.

### What was the percentage of unemployment in the USA in 1931 during the Depression?
In 1931, 15.9% of the workforce was unemployed.

### What was the percentage of unemployment in the USA in 1933 during the Depression?
In 1933, 24.9% of the workforce was unemployed.

### What was the percentage of unemployment in the USA in 1935 during the Depression?
In 1935, 20.1% of the workforce was unemployed.

### What was the percentage of unemployment in the USA in 1937 during the Depression?
In 1937, 14.3% of the workforce was unemployed.

### What was the percentage of unemployment in the USA in 1939 during the Depression?
In 1939, 19.0% of the workforce was unemployed.

### What was the percentage of unemployment in the USA in 1941 during the Depression?
In 1941, 9.9% of the workforce was unemployed.

---

**DID YOU KNOW?**

**Americans wrote hundreds of thousands of letters to Roosevelt.**

One voter wrote: "I am a long way from you in distance, yet my faith is in you, my heart with you, and I am for you, sink or swim."

# GLOSSARY

## A

**Abolish, Abolished** - to stop something, or get rid of it.

**Agnostic** - someone who takes the philosophical and religious stance that they do not, or can not, know the truth of the existence of God.

**Agricultural** - relating to agriculture.

**Agriculture** - an umbrella term to do with farming, growing crops or raising animals.

**Allies** - parties working together for a common objective, such as countries involved in a war. In both world wars, 'Allies' refers to those countries on the side of Great Britain.

**Anarchism** - the belief all government and organisation of society should be abolished.

**Anti-Semitic** - to be against, or hostile to, Jews.

**Assassinate** - to murder someone, usually an important figure, often for religious or political reasons.

**Assembly** - a meeting of a group of people, often as part of a country's government, to make decisions.

## B

**Bankrupt** - to be insolvent; to have run out of resources with which to pay existing debts.

**Boycott** - a way of protesting or bringing about change by refusing to buy something or use services.

**Bribe, Bribery, Bribes** - to dishonestly persuade someone to do something for you in return for money or other inducements.

## C

**Campaign** - a political movement to get something changed; in military terms, it refers to a series of operations to achieve a goal.

**Catholic** - a Christian who belongs to the Roman Catholic Church.

**Cavalry** - the name given to soldiers who fight on horseback.

**Claim** - someone's assertion of their right to something - for example, a claim to the throne.

**Communism** - the belief, based on the ideas of Karl Marx, that all people should be equal in society without government, money or private property. Everything is owned by by the people, and each person receives according to need.

**Communist** - a believer in communism.

**Conservative** - someone who dislikes change and prefers traditional values. It can also refer to a member of the Conservative Party.

**Constitution** - rules, laws or principles that set out how a country is governed.

**Constitutional** - relating to the constitution.

**Consumer goods** - products that people buy.

**Corrupt** - when someone is willing to act dishonestly for their own personal gain.

**Credit** - the ability to borrow money, or use goods or services, on the understanding that it will be paid for later.

**Culture** - the ideas, customs, and social behaviour of a particular people or society.

**Currency** - an umbrella term for any form of legal tender, but most commonly referring to money.

## D

**Debt** - when something, usually money, is owed by a person, organisation or institution to another.

**Democracy** - a political system where a population votes for its government on a regular basis. The word is Greek for 'the rule of people' or 'people power'.

**Deport** - to expel someone from a country and, usually, return them to their homeland.

**Dictator** - a ruler with absolute power over a country, often acquired by force.

**Discriminate, Discrimination** - to treat a person or group of people differently and in an unfair way.

## E

**Economic** - relating to the economy; also used when justifying something in terms of profitability.

**Economy** - a country, state or region's position in terms of production and consumption of goods and services, and the supply of money.

**Electrification** - Bringing electricity to places that previously did not have it.

**Empire** - a group of states or countries ruled over and controlled by a single monarch.

**Evolution** - a theory by Charles Darwin suggesting human beings developed slowly from other animals, such as apes.

**Export** - to transport goods for sale to another country.

**Extreme** - furthest from the centre or any given point. If someone holds extreme views, they are not moderate and are considered radical.

## F

**Fasting** - to deliberately refrain from eating, and often drinking, for a period of time.

**Federal** - in US politics this means 'national', referring to the whole country rather than any individual state.

**Foreign policy** - a government's strategy for dealing with other nations.

## G

# GLOSSARY

Ghetto - part of a city, often a slum area, occupied by a minority group.

## H

Hire purchase - a system where goods can be bought and paid for with a deposit and instalments over a period of time.

## I

Illiterate - unable to read or write.

Immigrant - someone who moves to another country.

Immigration - the act of coming to a foreign country with the intention of living there permanently.

Impeach, Impeachment - to charge someone, usually a high-ranking government official, with treason or a crime against the state.

Import - to bring goods or services into a different country to sell.

Independence, Independent - to be free of control, often meaning by another country, allowing the people of a nation the ability to govern themselves.

Industrial - related to industry, manufacturing and/or production.

Industrialisation, Industrialise, Industrialised - the process of developing industry in a country or region where previously there was little or none.

Industry - the part of the economy concerned with turning raw materials into into manufactured goods, for example making furniture from wood.

Inferior - lower in rank, status or quality.

Innovate, Innovation - the introduction and development of new things, such as inventions, methods or ideas.

Integrate - to bring people or groups with specific characteristics or needs into equal participation with others; to merge one thing with another to form a single entity.

Interpretation, Interpretations - a perceived meaning or particular explanation of something.

Investor - someone who puts money into something with the expectation of future profit.

## J

Juries, Jury - a group of people sworn to listen to evidence on a legal case and then deliver an impartial verdict based on what they have heard.

## L

Laissez-faire - the idea a government should take a hands-off approach to matters such as public health or the free market; it translates from the French as 'let it be'.

Left wing - used to describe political groups or individuals with beliefs that are usually centered around socialism and the idea of reform.

Legislature - The organisation or set of people who have the power to create laws.

Lynch, Lynched, Lynching - the killing of someone by a group of people for an alleged offence without a legal trial, usually publicly and often by hanging.

## M

Malnutrition - lack of proper nutrition caused by not eating enough of the right things or not having enough to eat. It can also be caused by the body not being able to use the food that is eaten.

Mass - an act of worship in the Catholic Church.

Mechanisation - Where human workers are replaced by machines or robots.

Middle class - refers to the socio-economic group which includes people who are educated and have professional jobs, such as teachers or lawyers.

Minister - a senior member of government, usually responsible for a particular area such as education or finance.

Modernise - to update something to make it suitable for modern times, often by using modern equipment or modern ideas.

Morals - a person's set of rules about what they consider right and wrong, used to guide their actions and behaviour.

## N

Nationalisation - the transfer of control or ownership of a sector of industry, such as banking or rail, from the private sector to the state.

## P

Persecute - to treat someone unfairly because of their race, religion or political beliefs.

Population - the number of people who live in a specified place.

Poverty - the state of being extremely poor.

Prejudice - prejudgement - when you assume something about someone based on a feature like their religion or skin colour, rather than knowing it as fact.

President - the elected head of state of a republic.

Prevent, Preventative, Preventive - steps taken to stop something from happening.

Proclamation - a public or official announcement of great importance.

Production - a term used to describe how much of something is made, for example saying a factory has a high production rate.

Profit - generally refers to financial gain; the amount of money made after deducting buying, operating or production costs.

Prosecute - to institute or conduct legal proceedings against a person or organisation.

Prosperity - the state of thriving, enjoying good fortune and/or social status.

# GLOSSARY

Protestant - someone belonging to the branch of the Christian Church that separated from the Roman Catholic Church in the 16th century.

## R

Radical, Radicalism - people who want complete or extensive change, usually politically or socially.

Raid - a quick surprise attack on the enemy.

Reform, Reforming - change, usually in order to improve an institution or practice.

Relief - something that reduces pressure on people, often through financial or practical support.

Repressive - a harsh or authoritarian action; usually used to describe governmental abuse of power.

Republic - a state or country run by elected representatives and an elected/nominated president. There is no monarch.

Reservation - an area of land given to Native Americans by the US government to keep them away from settlers.

Riots - violent disturbances involving a crowd of people.

## S

Segregation - when people are kept separately from each other - often used in the context of race.

Sharecropper - someone who farmed land belonging to a landowner in return for giving them a share of their crops.

Sin - in religion, an immoral act against God's laws.

Standard of living - level of wealth and goods available to an individual or group.

State, States - an area of land or a territory ruled by one government.

Strike - a refusal by employees to work as a form of protest, usually to bring about change in their working conditions. It puts pressure on their employer, who cannot run the business without workers.

Suburban - An outer area of a city, usually where houses are less tightly packed in.

Suppress, Suppression - the use of force to stop something, such as a protest.

## T

Tariff, Trade tariff - a tax placed on imports, increasing their cost.

Trade unions - organised groups of workers who cooperate to make their lives better at work. For example, they might negotiate for better pay and then organise a strike if one is refused.

Treason - the crime of betraying one's country, often involving an attempt to overthrow the government or kill the monarch.

## U

U-boat - the German name for a submarine.

Unconstitutional - not in accordance with the constitution of a country or organisation.

Upper class - a socio-economic group consisting of the richest people in a society who are wealthy because they own land or property.

## V

Veto - the right to reject a decision or proposal.

## W

WASP - white Anglo-Saxon Protestant.

Welfare - wellbeing; often refers to money and services given to the poorest people.

White supremacist - one who believes white people are superior to people of other ethnicities and should therefore be dominant.

# INDEX

## A
Advertising, 1920s - *21*
African Americans, 1920s - *43*
Alphabet Agencies - *63*
America in 1918 - *14*

## B
Bonus Army March - *58*

## C
Capone, Al - *51*
Car industry - *23*
Cinema, 1920s - *35*
Construction, 1920s - *22*
Consumer goods, 1920s - *24*
Consumerism - *25*
Coughlin, Father Charles - *67*
Credit - *24*
Cycle of prosperity - *18*

## D
Declining industries, 1920s - *28*
Depression, 1930s - *54*

## E
Economic boom, 1920s - *18*
Economic weaknesses, 1920s - *52*
Election, 1932 - *59*
Electricity - *26*
Entertainment, 1920s - *34*

## F
FDR - *59*
Farmers, 1920s - *30*
Farmers, 1930s - *55*
Fireside Chats - *60*
Flappers - *33*
Ford, Henry - *23*

## G
Government, 1920s - *28*
Government, US system - *15*
Great Depression, the - *54*

## H
Hoover, Herbert - *56*

## I
Immigration, 1920s - *38*
Inventions, 1920s - *21*

## J
Jazz, 1920s - *36*

## K
Ku Klux Klan - *44*

## L
Long, Huey - *67*

## M
Mass production - *22*

## N
New Deal - *60*
New Deal, opposition - *65*
New Deal, success - *69*

## P
Prohibition - *49*
Prosperity, cycle of - *18*

## R
Radio, 1920s - *37*
Red Scare, First - *40*
Religious divide, 1920s - *46*
Religious fundamentalism, 1920s - *47*
Religious modernism, 1920s - *47*
Roaring Twenties - *31*
Roosevelt, Franklin Delano - *59*

## S
Sacco-Vanzetti Case - *41*
Scopes Trial - *48*
Shares - *26*
Sinclair, Upton - *68*
Sport, 1920s - *35*

# INDEX

**Stock market** - *26*

## T

**Townsend, Doctor Frances** - *68*
**Travel, 1920s** - *37*

## U

**US election, 1932** - *59*
**US government, 1920s** - *28*
**US system of government** - *15*
**USA and WWI** - *16*
**USA, situation in 1918** - *14*
**Unemployment, 1930s** - *71*

## W

**WWI and USA** - *16*
**Wall Street Crash** - *53*
**Wall Street Crash, effects** - *54*
**Women, 1920s** - *32*

www.ingramcontent.com/pod-product-compliance
Lightning Source LLC
Chambersburg PA
CBHW050718090526
44588CB00014B/2333